And,
Still I Rise

WOMEN'S COMPILATION PROJECT

Volume 1

Featuring:

Sheila Baldwin-Williams
Bridget Burns-Diarrassouba
Marsha Clarke
Ms. Cynthia
Yolanda Dupree
Betty Efemini
Lisa Frank
Angela Patterson
Chenise Payton
Shirley Poitier
Phyllis Powell
Gabriela Rivero
Normia Vázquez Scales
Judith Watkins
Velma White

Published by
Again I Rise Publishing
Chicago, Illinois

Printed in the United States of America

ISBN: 978-0-9986148-0-9

Library of Congress Control Number: 2017901280

Cover and Interior Design by Jessica Tilles/TWA Solutions

All stories appear courtesy of the authors, unless otherwise noted.

Scriptures used are taken from the New King James Version Bible.

The Women's Compilation Project is hosted by Mutual Partners Association, which is nonprofit organization that implement after-school and summer programs for youth in urban communities. The proceeds from this book will help pay for youth to attend after-school and summer programs that teach character development, self-esteem, leadership skills and experiential learning through fun activities such as theater, music, art, dance and sports.

Acknowledgments

First and foremost, I would like to thank my Lord and Savior Jesus Christ for entrusting me with this project. Truly, without Him, none of this would have been possible. I would like to thank my mother, Mary Loretta Burns, for her love and support. You are an amazing woman who taught me to be a giver and to be loving and compassionate toward others. Mom, you have been my lifetime support system and I appreciate the love you show me daily. I love you with all my heart! I am very grateful to my husband, Abdoulaye Diarrassouba's, for his support, love, and daily encouragement. God truly blessed me the day we met. I would like to thank my late father, Leroy Tripplett, who always believed in me. Whenever I thought I could not do something, he would say, "Baby, you can do it." He was such a wonderful dad who taught me the philosophy of life and how to live life intentionally. I would like to thank my extended family as well for always supporting me in the many endeavors I have embarked upon; Lord knows I have done a few.

God has placed some of the most amazing people in my life. I would specifically like to thank all the women who have consistently supported The Experience Now® and The Girlfriend's Weekend Retreats. These women have been amazing and I truly consider all of them the sisters I never had. With deep gratitude, I would like to thank all the women who participated in The Women's Compilation Project. I do not take your participation lightly. You opened your hearts to this project and entrusted me throughout the process of creating this book. I know it's God's will and His divine order that we all have come together to contribute to something greater than ourselves. I am forever thankful for your obedience to God's call to participate in this project. I could not have done this without your loyalty and commitment.

In addition, I would like to thank my trusted mentor, Deborah Dillon, who inspired me many years ago to start my own business and in 2006, I made that dream a reality and started a nonprofit organization. I could not have done that without her guidance and motivation. Throughout the years, she has given me encouragement; I am thankful to have Deb in my life. Finally, I would be remiss not to mention my editor, Jessica Tilles, who worked tirelessly with me until we got this project just right.

Thank you all from the bottom of my heart.

Bridget Burns-Diarrassoba
Publisher

Table of Contents

≫ SHEILA BALDWIN-WILLIAMS ≪

Life Has Teachable Moments

≫ SHEILA BALDWIN-WILLIAMS ≪

Life Has Teachable Moments

*L*ife…four simple letters, each signifying immeasurable events and experiences we will encounter during our life span. Consequently, each encounter is comprised of teachable moments. Some moments are good, some bad, however, life does consist of teachable moments, with a lesson accompanying each one. Since each life span given, is given by the Creator of us all, a specified amount of time is allotted for experiences of all kinds we can learn from regardless of how and when it is presented. Therefore, I'm sharing my thoughts and lessons from my teachable moments with you; I hope you will be able to identify the lesson before you experience it because life is full of countless teachable moments.

Teachable Moments Defined

Teachable moments…how would you define these two words? My guess would be a clear-cut one. Seeing as the word "teachable" has the root word *teach* within it, my summation of a definition is, "an individual is able to receive teaching." Next, moments consist of different intervals of time within any given point of the day. In configuring both words, my conjecture for the words together, "teachable moments," consist of the following, "an individual able to receive teaching at different intervals of time within any given point of the day."

This definition definitely transpires on a daily basis from the time an individual is able to comprehend. Childhood is definitely where it all begins…

So, Life Begins

My journey began in the North Shore suburbs of Chicago, Illinois, where I was born to a young married couple from the South. My mother always had a way of making me think. I guess my grandmother did, too, for that matter. I still remember her sweet little southern ways today, and I'm quite sure my mom transferred some of her teachings on to my siblings and me as well. Some individuals have children, but cease to take time to engage in raising, training, and preparing them for life. This was not the case with mother, grandmother, and my other family members.

#1 Guard Your Mouth

I learned not to engage in conversations with adults unless invited to do so. Why was that the case? I didn't understand then, however now I can't tolerate a child's input in the conversation I may have with an adult. I sum it up as a teachable moment from childhood. My mother's infamous statement when I was a child was, "A child should stay in a child's place…" Now that's a teachable moment and there were other moments as well.

Lesson Learned

"Children should act and remain as children,
adulthood will occur soon enough."
—Coach Sheila

#2 Money and Banking

I recall going for a car ride one Saturday with my mother. The destination was unknown, but that was okay because I was happy being out with my mother. I had finished babysitting that day, which was my first introduction to working and earning money. Well, turns out we ended up at the neighborhood bank with my mother opening up a bank account for me. I still laugh at it now but she only taught me how to fill out a deposit ticket! How awesome is that? A deposit ticket and not a withdrawal ticket which I learned how to fill out later on my own.

Lesson Learned

Now that I'm an adult, a quote by Dave Ramsey speaks volumes to me, he says,
"You have to teach children about money intentionally—create teachable moments."
I believe train a child in the manner he or she will be able to reflect on later in years to come.

"Creating teachable moments are something all children need. It prepares them for being productive and successful adults later in life."
—Coach Sheila

More Years of Learning

Growing up wasn't always easy. There were times when our home life had storms in the midst of it, but through it all, I learned to adjust and get through each one as they came. For instance, growing up with a weekend alcoholic father, who worked hard every day, but became intoxicated beginning on Thursdays, which was his payday. As a child I witnessed this ritual every week and knew exactly what to expect, better yet, what I didn't want for my life. Regardless of the scenario, teachable moments come in diverse ways.

Relationships
#3 Examples Set Before You

While growing up within my parent's home, there were countless teachable moments while observing my father whom I thought I had a great deal of hate for, only later to discover it was only hurt. May he now rest in peace; I thank God our relationship was an awesome one during the latter portion of his life. He loved me, I loved him, and it gets no better than that. Prior to his passing on, the Lord used me to rededicate his life back to Christ. In observing the old him, I discovered what I didn't want in a spouse; an alcoholic, functioning or not.

Although my father's drinking instilled qualities I knew not to engage in, I ascertained the character of a man is extremely important when embarking on marriage. At some point during marriage, children arrive. Parents should desire to impart into their children standards such as possessing a good character, integrity, reverence for God, and positive values to live by to name a few. Each marriage without any qualm, experience teachable moments. However, one important thing to remember is example is set before our children following our footsteps towards marriage.

Lesson Learned

"Pay close attention to character examples
presented to you so you will know what you do
and do not want to allow during the duration of
your life. Examples are all around us, pay close
attention..."—Coach Sheila

#4 Working Relationships

I recall a time when I felt like I was being unjustly persecuted on my job. I took a stand to change my lifestyle from going out to happy hour after work with coworkers. I was faced with a lot of alienation. What a storm and teachable moment! I got through it by standing up for my beliefs. As a result, I ended up promoted to another position within another building away from the madness. I held my ground and soon enough, the storm was over.

Each storm has taught me how to be strong and wait the storms of life out. If anything, I learned storms don't last forever, eventually the sun is going to resurface and shine brightly again. So, what am I saying here? I'm saying to be patient when life deals you a fist full of trouble...trouble may come, but it doesn't last forever. Be willing to make adjustments that can better your circumstances instead of complaining and doing nothing about them at all. I looked for other ways out and utilized my church as a way to stay focused.

Lesson Learned

"Church can be that vehicle that transports you
from the troubles storm brings in your life to
having peace in the midst of the storm."
—Coach Sheila

Church and Spirituality

I was introduced to church early in my life, although there were times I veered to the left, somehow, some way, I have always managed to get back on the right path. At first, church was a way to escape, a way to hang out with my family and friends. Sure, I had participated in the children's choir when I was a youngster, the usher ministry, and even became president of the young people's department at some point during my teenage years. Did I have a real relationship with the Lord? Now I now know what a real one should be.

Unfortunately, this is something that occurs a great deal within different churches of different faiths globally. I call it practicing religion but not having a true relationship with the Creator, the Lord God Himself. The Bible says it this way in 2 Timothy 2:5 NLT, "They will act religious, but they will reject the power that could make them godly. Stay away from people like that!" Thank God, this is no longer who I am.

#5 The Real Thing

Well, eventually my practicing religion turned into the real thing! This brings to mind the old Coke slogan "Ain't nothing like the real thing"! You can't stay in the church, surround yourself with true born again believers and not experience the new spiritual birth. Yes, I became born again. I experienced an awakening so real in my spirit that I'm still going through new awakenings today. There have been a few times over the past thirty-two years I have strayed a little bit to the left during my journey and walk, but God was and still is right here with me. He promises all born again believers can embrace and have faith to believe He means what he says. Deuteronomy 31:8 ESV says, "It is the LORD who goes before you. He will be with you; he will not leave you or forsake you. Do not fear or be dismayed." This scripture verse has sustained me during my walk and has caused me to live the life of a real born again believer. The experience has genuinely been real!

Lesson Learned

"You can play but you will pay with your life
if you're not truly born again in God."
—Coach Sheila

Final Thoughts

I have shared just a mere smidgen of my experiences in hopes someone will be able to identify with teachable moments when they occur. An individual will travel numerous paths during a life span. From birth to adulthood examples an individual will experience can consist in the realm of finances, relationships, employment, spirituality, and countless more that can present moments of lessons learned. Sometimes the lesson is never learned. As a result, an individual may find himself or herself repeating the same vicious cycle of learning how to be teachable until eventually, the teachings become learned ones and not repeatable ones.

Repeating a cycle of what should be learned, teachable moments can cause conflicts, uneasiness, waste of time, or low self-esteem if you recognize, but don't completely know how to correct your actions. The cycle can progress on for many wasted years until an end resolve is finally apprehended. I know, I've been there on a few occasions, which is why I'm able to share a few experiences to with others. Always remember what you view and do in life can result in life having teachable moments—view and do carefully. Finally, as Michelle Landy says, "Live with a teachable spirit."

Sheila Baldwin-Williams understands very well that the journey of life has countless twist and turns to it, and along the journey, changes usually occur, and lessons are learned. Because of her array of experiences in life, she often uses them as tools to help others. This is why she enjoys being an agent of change to many seeking change for their life. Functioning as an Ordained Minister, Certified Life Coach, Educator, Mentor, and Author, she has been coined the "Destiny Changer" by many of her clients.

Sheila Baldwin-Williams has received a Master of Science in Psychology, Bachelor of Science in Business Management and is a New Life Coach Inc. Certified Christian Life Coach graduate. She is a business entrepreneur and Founder and Leader of The Daughters of Issachar Ministries. She resides in the Atlanta, Georgia area with her husband and family.

≫ BRIDGET BURNS-DIARRASSOUBA ≪

Obeying the Voice of God

Obeying the Voice of God

Waking abruptly, I sat straight up in bed, my heart thumping. I looked into the darkness and listened for what might have woken me up. There was no sound coming from Remy's room. I peered at the alarm clock on the bedside table. It was three in the morning. I sighed and wondered why this had happened so frequently for the last six months.

I nestled under the covers and shut my eyes, trying to go back to sleep. My brain was too alert. It was like an impossible task. I threw the covers off me. *I might as well look in on Remy*, I thought, although there was no real reason to do so. He was a good sleeper, other than the first night when he had called out in his sleep. His room was opposite mine and I left both doors open. If he so much as made a sound, I would hear him.

He lay sprawled on the bed, his right hand hanging over the edge. I tiptoed in and arranged the covers around him. I sat on the edge of his bed and took in his mass of curls that made me want to ruffle his hair. He was the best thing that had happened to me and the last five months had been the happiest in my life.

Sometimes, I found it hard to believe he was my son, but I had the adoption papers to prove it. I had longed for a child of my own for as long as I could remember. I had waited and prayed for the right man to come into my life, but he just hadn't come along. However, I didn't want to abandon my dream of being a mother. Remy was the answer to my prayer. I had always longed to adopt a child, knowing how many children in the world needed a safe, loving home.

This was why these episodes of waking up at three in the morning did not make sense. I was happy and contented. I didn't understand why sleep evaded me at three in the morning.

Remy had filled that void in my heart and the emptiness in my life. I looked forward to leaving work to pick him up at the preschool he attended. There was so much to thank the Lord for.

I sighed, planted a light kiss on the back of his head, and crept out of the room.

For the next couple of hours, I could not go back to sleep. By the time I fell asleep, it was time to get up.

"You look tired lately," my co-worker Kesha said to me that morning, her brown eyes filled with concern.

"I know. I have been waking up every morning at three o'clock and I can't go back to sleep afterwards."

"Is there something on your mind?"

I shook my head. "Nothing at all."

She held my arm gently. "Have you thought that perhaps the Lord is trying to speak to you?"

Puzzled, I waited for her to say more.

"Remember the story of Samuel? 1 Samuel 3?"

I nodded, but I couldn't make the connection. God had distinctly called out to Samuel by his name. In my case, there was nothing but an inability to go back to sleep.

"The Lord called Samuel three times in his sleep. Prophet Eli told him to answer and listen to what the Lord wanted to say to him."

My heart pounded. "You think the Lord is speaking to me?"

Kesha shrugged. "It's possible. The next time you wake up at three, why not pray and listen for God's voice?"

It happened the very following morning. Again, I woke up with the feeling that something had awakened me. I got out of bed and knelt down.

"Dear Lord, thank you for my life and every blessing you've bestowed on me. I'm your humble servant," I prayed, my voice shaking.

I was silent, as Kesha had suggested, and in that moment, I could feel the Lord's presence in my room.

Do you Love Me, Bridget?

My eyes popped open and I looked around the room, frantically. There was no one, yet the question had been as clear as if God was speaking right into my ear. I shut my eyes. I had loved the Lord all my life and had strived to live in a way that pleased Him.

"Yes, Lord, I love you," I answered in a strong, sure voice.

"Go and serve my people," God said. "Feed ten hungry people."

I waited, but He said no more. I prayed, more fervently than I ever had. Questions nagged my mind. Had I truly heard God's voice or had it been my imagination?

"Dear Lord, please show me that it was You I heard...that You spoke to me," I pleaded.

I needed more. Feeling emotionally exhausted, I got up and picked up my Bible. I opened it at random, with no particular scripture in mind. My eyes fell on a verse. Isaiah 58:7.

"Share your food with the hungry and open your homes to the homeless poor. Give clothes to those who have nothing to wear, and do not refuse to help your own relatives."

Peace descended into my heart. "Thank you, Lord," I whispered.

I woke up the following morning, feeling the weight of what had transpired during the night. How would I even begin to obey the Lord? My legs and knees felt weak. Images flashed through my mind. The homeless man who stood for hours on the corner, cursing people and throwing things as they hurried past. I shivered at the thought of speaking to such a man.

We lived near the Somerset complex for homeless people. Most of them were mentally ill and frightened me. They roamed the neighborhood, insulting people and even urinating out in the open. I steered clear of them and kept an eye out, to avoid running into one of them while I was out.

It was my day off from work. I dropped Remy off at preschool and went to the grocery store to buy lunch meat and bread. Once home, I went straight into the kitchen. I refused to think too much. I would obey God, despite the many misgivings I had. Still, my hands trembled as I made the sandwiches, but I kept going.

I packed the ten sandwiches and, with a heavy spirit, I left the house and headed for the park where I knew there would be many homeless people. In the park, I stood with a rigid posture, my muscles tense and my clammy hands gripping the bag with sandwiches.

"Lord, if You told me to do this, You have to help me," I said under my breath.

Before ten seconds had passed, a man in tattered, dirty clothes approached me.

"Ma'am, you have a sandwich in that bag?"

How did he know? I thought, while handing him the sandwich. Before I could get out the park, I had given away all ten sandwiches. I left the park overwhelmed with gratitude. I had no more doubts that the Lord had spoken to me. I now knew my calling and though I had no idea how I would afford to feed the homeless with my paycheck, I believed the Lord would make a way.

The following week, I prepared sandwiches to feed twenty-five people. As had happened the previous week, homeless people came up to me and asked me for a sandwich. The next week, I fed fifty people and after that, the number soared to a hundred. My mom was a big help. I would drop the food off to her on my way home and when I returned, the sandwiches were made. Sometimes we had extras, like cookies.

One evening, I went to bed at the usual time, my heart heavy. I had no money to buy food for the homeless people who had come to depend on me for their midevening meals. They knew me by name and would wait patiently. I imagined the disappointment they would feel when I did not show up. In the morning, I woke up and got ready for the day without knowing how I would feed the homeless in the park.

Then, a knock came at the door. It was Georgia, an older woman in her seventies who lived next door, but whom I was not particularly close to. I was surprised to see her at that time of morning. She went straight into the reason she had come.

"I was praying this morning and the Lord came to me. He directed me to come to you and ask what you need," she said.

I was stunned and it took a moment to gather myself. I explained to Georgia what I had been doing with the homeless people and how I had no money that day to buy what I needed to make the sandwiches.

"How much do you need?"

"Sixty dollars."

She went back home and returned moments later with sixty dollars. My joy knew no bounds. The only day I did not have money to feed the homeless and the Lord provided. It reminded me of a vision I had when I was eight years old. It had remained etched in my mind.

The Lord told me I would have struggles in my life, but if I obeyed Him and always have faith in Him, my latter days would be better than my former. He was right. My life had gotten better and more fulfilled than I could have ever imagined. No matter how difficult things got, that episode with Georgia reinforced to me how important it was to have faith in God.

I was floored at the goodness of the Lord. I kept going for a year and then two. I still harbored dreams of meeting a good man and getting married, but I hadn't met anyone. One morning, I woke up with a feeling of loneliness. I had prayed to meet someone, but it hadn't happened. I sat perched on the bed and then slid down to my knees.

"I give up, Lord. Maybe it's not part of Your plan for me to meet someone. I accept that I will be single all my life," I prayed, my heart aching and my spirits low.

I had made plans to visit my mother that day and after a breakfast of pancakes, Remy and I got ready. By that time, I had returned to my usual cheerful self. You could not be low in spirits with Remy there. He was a ray of sunlight, with tales of school and his friends. When I adopted him, I named him Remy because in some part of Africa, Remy meant to take away a mother's tears. That is just what he did for me. He was at that age where he asked loads of questions and we could talk for hours.

"I have to fill up the car," I said to Remy and turned off the main road.

A very dark man was in front, and glanced at me several times as he filled up his car. Our eyes met and I quickly looked away, heat rising from my neck. When he was done, he came walking toward me. He had kind eyes and a gentle manner of speaking. He smiled, and I smiled back.

"May I take you out to dinner one of these days?" he asked, his eyes never leaving mine.

I nodded. "Maybe."

"Well, here's my number. Call me if you are interested."

I took his number and hummed a tune all the way to my mother's house.

I called him exactly a week later, having debated for hours if I really wanted to get my hopes up again. I would play it by ear, I decided. He took Remy and I to a very nice restaurant and we all had a wonderful time. After that, Mike became a part of our lives, and though he was not actively involved at first in my feeding the homeless, he supported me. Eight months later, Mike proposed and I knew the Lord had answered my prayer.

Our lives continued and so did my ministry. We were happy and living that family life I had always prayed for.

My journey had taught me it is not always easy to obey God. It's very hard; Satan will sometimes use fear to keep you away from what God has called you to do. If we choose with our wills to obey, despite the difficulties, it will always pay off in the end. I am a living testimony. Following God's path has opened a world of fulfillment, joy, and opportunities that I could have never imagined.

Bridget Burns-Diarrassouba

Bridget Burns-Diarrassouba is a certified Christian Life Coach and founder of New Life Coach Inc, a nonprofit organization dedicated to providing free life coaching to those who are unable to afford such services. Bridget has a heart for helping people and regularly serves the homeless population providing food, clothing and other essential needs. Bridget is also the founder of the Women's Compilation Book Project. In her free time she enjoys volunteering, mentoring women in the area of finding their purpose, and spending time with her family and friends.

※ MARSHA CLARKE ※

As Much As Things Have Changed

As Much As Things Have Changed

*S*ecretary Hillary Clinton didn't stand a chance in hell of winning Florida. As an African American woman, who grew up in the South, in a small town forty-five miles north of Tampa, I know Florida is one of the most racist and sexist states in America.

My family life revolved around the Black community. I lived in one, attended a church for Blacks and the community center was for Blacks. This was in the sixties when Blacks lived in one part of town and the Whites lived in another. The one part of my life that actively involved Whites was the White school I attended.

I came from a middle class family who had done well for themselves and was greatly respected in the Black community. My great grandfather was the founder and owner of the church I attended as a child, and my grandmother and her siblings owned several businesses in the community.

Though my grandparents and their siblings had not gone past high school, their children and grandchildren graduated from Florida A&M University, a historically Black college located in Tallahassee.

Black families were so much closer in those days and they did everything they could to help each other. My great grandfather owned a sprawling house, fondly called 'The Big House', and all my uncles and aunts stayed there until they were able to purchase homes of their own.

Because of my great grandfather's respect in the community and relationships with the White bankers, my family had their loans easily approved. Despite his standing and the standing of other upright Blacks, segregation was very much a part of life for Black people.

At the time, there was one school for Blacks, from elementary through high school. Everything Black folks needed, such as barbershops, grocery stores, churches, and community centers were found in the community where they resided. There was really no reason, other than work, to leave the community.

Fast forward to the sixties when I was growing up—racial lines had become sharper. My mother, Bennie Mae, together with my grandmother, Clyde, loved one other thing, apart from cooking. They loved beautiful clothes and they found these in an exclusive boutique called Rogers', whose patrons were the wealthy folk of Brooksville, and surrounding areas. I remember the compliments I received every Sunday about my unique pretty dresses. It's no wonder I grew up thinking we were rich folk. I must admit, I was pretty spoiled.

My mother was an educator and highly regarded. She and my father, Ernest, drove fancy cars, owned properties as well as their own home, and I lacked for nothing. It was an ideal childhood and as I blossomed into a young woman, developing these same relationships as my mother had, I bought my clothes in the same exclusive boutique on my mother's tab.

You would be forgiven for thinking the city was progressive, right? Hardly. Across the road from Rogers' boutique, a stone's throw away, was a restaurant that did not allow Blacks to walk in through the front doors. There was a separate side entrance for Colored patrons. My mother had warned me never to go into that restaurant, as she had a rule, we did not visit establishments we could not walk through the front door because of the color of our skin.

My mother also forbade me to go to a grocery store on the same block that allowed Blacks to get groceries on credit. Although credit was extended the interest rates on that credit was ridiculously high, according to those who did shop there. My mother did not believe in buying grocery on credit and she did not like the assumption that our people only bought things on credit. Though we stayed away from such establishments, I was aware they existed.

As much as we were doing well as a family, as a Black community, we were very much segregated. Every three to four years, the KKK would hold a rally on the steps of the courthouse. In defense, the NAACP would stand on the other side of the steps. The parents of some of the White kids, whom I attended school with, were members of the KKK, but I don't recall being openly discriminated against.

A memory etched in my mind of those days, was of a group of White boys driving big four-wheel trucks to school, flying confederate flags. There was never a confrontation with the White kids at school and, in fact, I had some great friends who were White. I had two really good white girlfriends in high school who spent nights at my house and I at their houses and never felt any discrimination.

Though, in the back of my mind, I knew when the rubber met the road, if they had to choose a side, they would side with their group. Life was good for me, but the KKK, with their white costumes, as well as the segregation of Blacks and Whites, left an indelible mark on me.

In following with my family's tradition, I attended Florida A&M University (FAMU) after graduating high school. FAMU, being a historically Black college, changed my view of the world. I viewed my mother, aunts and uncles through a different lens and I understood them better. My experience at FAMU taught me who I was and where I fitted into the world. The Black experience was infused into the studies so I gained a completely new insight into our community. My aim, after my studies, was to move to a city where the majority of the population was Black.

I moved to Washington, DC, otherwise known as Chocolate City. There, I was on a steep learning curve. Living in a city where the majority of people were Blacks was a completely different life. As my experiences widened, I read widely, watched the news, and visited Florida, I reached the conclusion that my home state was a racist state. I had my education to thank for that.

Education allows a person to deal with issues from a point of experience and knowledge rather than emotion.

The very people I grew up with, and have known all my life, showed their real colors when the first African American President was sworn in to the highest office of the land. I suppose I had known they were racist, but I had always given them the benefit of the doubt. Like many people, I hadn't realized just how racist Florida, and the rest of the country, was until an African American President was elected.

Florida is not only racist, but it's also a sexist state. The school of thought was that girls should be seen and not heard. Many of the White girls got married after graduating from high school, vowing to remain as stay-at-home moms. It was expected of them and they were more than happy to fit into the mold. Very few sought professional careers or pursued higher educational opportunities.

As Much As Things Have Changed

The counties neighboring my hometown of Brooksville, Florida, overwhelmingly voted for Trump in this election. After they had gotten their very first African American President, there was no way they would have voted for a woman, even a White woman. The standards and expectations were much lower for Trump than for Clinton.

Women are still unable to crash through that glass ceiling. There will always be double standards when it comes to the most qualified, and standards are never equal. My education and experiences would not allow me to tolerate racism and sexism, whether subtle or blatant, and I lost many friends during the election.

As much as things have changed, the truth is that they have pretty much stayed the same. Whereas there are no signs for 'Colored' people or KKK meetings on the steps of the courthouse, racism is very much alive, albeit subtle now. Property owners are known to write 'C' on applications, identifying the applicant as Colored. This is to avoid renting property to Black people. African Americans are no longer denied loans. Instead, they are given sub-prime loans with unaffordable interest rates, leading to foreclosures.

No longer are dogs and water hoses unleashed on innocent crowds of African Americans, but innocent, unarmed African Americans are killed by the police, the very people who ought to be protecting them, at alarming rates. There are no more registries used to track the sale of African Americans, however, our prisons are overflowing with people of color.

What can we do to change our racist and sexist society? We must develop a strategic plan that addresses our day-to-day needs. The first thing we must do to change our society is to hold our local officials accountable. When they do not fulfill their role, we must vote them out. We must not accept mediocre performance or a lackluster approach to responsibility in the officials' we have voted into office.

Secondly, we must understand how the political process works, as well as the importance of our individual votes. As a society that badly needs change, our right to vote is our voice for the change we want to see in society. As African Americans, who make up a large voting block, we must elect candidates who will address issues that disturb us such as police brutality against African Americans.

The third thing we must do is to save our money. Money is power, and without it, you give away your power. Research has shown that a majority of African Americans does not have a culture of saving money or investing. We must make a decision to eradicate poverty as individuals and as a community. Financial freedom means, as a community, our focus will shift once we are free of debt, to climbing bigger mountains that will, in the long term, eradicate racism and sexism.

We must support and buy Black. We can no longer wait for someone to save or empower us. We must do it ourselves. Rather than buying your everyday goods and services from large corporations or chain stores, choose to purchase from an African American-owned store or company. It might be an inconvenience and time consuming, but the ripple effect can change the economy of African Americans. More people would be able to grow their businesses and, in turn, employ more people, which would mean less idle people and lower crime rates. Our businesses cannot succeed without help from us. The stronger our businesses become, the less we become dependent upon or be controlled by other folk.

Reading empowers people. As African Americans, we must become fervent readers. Our horizons will expand, we will have a greater understanding of ourselves and our society, and our minds will expand so we can see solutions to our problems. Reading creates awareness of one's surroundings and new insights into situations.

By becoming fervent readers, we will have a deeper understanding of the issues that affect us as a community, and find ways to improve our economic power as well as demand for the recognition of our rights as citizens of a democratic society. As readers, our children and the generations that follow will become readers, thus ending ignorance and illiteracy in the generations to come.

Finally, we must pray without ceasing. The Bible says, *"The effectual fervent prayer of a righteous man availeth much."* We cannot get discouraged by the subtle racism we see everywhere around us. That verse promises us that our prayers are effective and powerful, and we shall one day see the results of our prayers.

We cannot sit and wait for the change we wish to see, or hope other people will do it for us. If each one of us made the decision to change our society by taking the actionable steps stated in the previous paragraphs, with time, racism, whether blatant or subtle, will decrease. African American lives, dreams, and goals will matter. It is time to be the change that we want to see!

Marsha Clarke is a business consultant and certified Christian Life Coach dedicated to helping her clients find renewed purpose in their personal, professional, and spiritual lives. Marsha is currently pursuing her PhD in Nonprofit Management with an emphasis on executive leadership attainment for African American women. In her free time, she enjoys reading and research. Marsha Clarke B.S., M.B.A., Ph.D. (c)

My 9/11 Horror

My 9/11 Horror

*T*his is a difficult piece for me to write, as it was the most painful time in my life. I hope that sharing my experience will help someone else. Sometimes, life can be a difficult experience. All of us will experience overwhelming hurt at some point in life. Because Jesus Christ walked with me, I survived my pain. My experience might be unpleasant for some, but what I endured may help you to put your pain into perspective. Matthew 5:45 (KJV) says, *"for he maketh his sun to rise on the evil and on the good, and sendeth rain on the just and on the unjust."*

It all began in 1984 when I was a bus operator for the Chicago Transit Authority. I worked the "swing" shift. I started work at 7:30 a.m. and ended at 9:30 a.m., followed by a "fallback," which you could say was an extended lunch anywhere from two to four hours, and then I worked four hours more. My routine was regular. After pulling the bus into the garage at 9:30 a.m., I would have quiet time with my devotions. No one would be around, so I could pray and read my Bible.

One day, I was in deep prayer and I felt the presence of the Lord. I was lying on the long side seat of the bus, and low and behold, the Lord was sitting at the steering wheel. Some people would have been afraid, but I wasn't afraid because, at Bible study the night before, the pastor told us about a vision he had of a man sitting on the edge of his bed. He said, "Don't be afraid if you have an experience like that." So, I wasn't because the pastor prepared me for it. He didn't say he was Jesus, but I knew he was. "Lord," I said, still as a rock.

"I will show you the great things thou will suffer for my namesake," he said, and just as he came, he left.

I had no idea of what he was saying!

Many times, people say, "God never speaks to us," but he does speak. Often, we just do not make time to hear him. Jesus will never compete with all the things you have going on in your life. You have to make time to be with him. Jesus honors faithfulness, determination, and love. When you make him your priority, he will make you his priority. He says in Revelations 3:20 (KJV), *"Behold, I stand at the door, and knock: if any man hear my voice, and open the door, I will come in to him, and I will sup with him, and he with me."* Jesus is always knocking at the door of your heart, but it's up to you to let him in.

One night, I was working on Archer Avenue, and a passenger and I were talking about Job from the Old Testament. The person was talking about how Job suffered; he lost everything he had and all of his children and God allowed it to happen. After the passenger left the bus the story of Job remained in my mind for some strange reason. I thought, maybe it's because I was going through some painful issues at that time. But later, I found the story of Job hitting close to home.

Fast forward Seventeen Years Later

In 2001, I drove an eighteen-wheeler, and my boss and I didn't get along. On July 1, 2001, while at work, I went to start my truck and the dispatcher called me into the office and handed me a letter. A letter of termination stating I had too many accidents and the company couldn't insure me. Bam! No job. I went home and tried to think. I only had one accident, but the letter stated "too many." When could you be uninsurable because of one accident? It made no sense. The next day, I applied for unemployment. The following day, I started looking for another job. It was the reasonable thing to do, right? You move on.

The employment office sent me a letter, stating I needed to come in and see a deputy. The deputy said the trucking company was refusing to give me unemployment because I had torn up their truck. I was astonished. "tore up what truck?" I asked. I was furious at this point. The company fired me, and now they were lying to try to keep me from getting unemployment. "No way José," I told the deputy if that were true, there had to be an accident report or report of repaired damages on a specific date. They couldn't prove it with reports, so the deputy awarded me my claim.

I kept applying for work, but I wasn't getting any responses. Companies hire truck drivers almost on the spot. All you have to do is show up. I returned to one business and asked if there was a problem; I found out my former employer was telling potential job prospects that I wrecked their truck. I filed an EEOC complaint that drug on forever.

Then the big bombshell happened sometime between losing my job in July and August 1. I was in the house alone. Many times I wouldn't have on the TV, or the radio because the Lord was disciplining me in being alone with him. It is in isolation that God will speak. He will answer prayers, heal, deliver, and set free. One morning, while in devotion,

The Lord said, "Art, your son, is going to die!"

"Oh God! help me!" I cried. "Lord, I don't even know where my son is, please. Don't let him die and I don't know where he is! Oh God, help me!" After, receiving that message I couldn't tell this to anyone at the time.

Eight days later, I was over to my ex-husband's house with my daughter who lived with her father. Cook County Corrections called. Art had been in a domestic violence incident. The woman asked if they could send him into my custody.

I told her, "Oh no!"

I thought if he stayed in jail, maybe he would live. Instead, they released him on an I-bond.

On August 30, 2001, I was talking to a Vietnam Veteran, who was still upset about the men he saw die in battle.

"You should be on your knees thanking God you made it," I told him.

Then the Lord said, "Tell him I, alone, decide who will live and who will die."

The next day, August 31 at 6:00 p.m., Northwestern Hospital called. The doctor spoke so harshly. He asked if I was Cynthia Lucas.

"Yes."

"Your son is here, and he's dead!"

Oh, my God! I called his uncle, Joe, to come and take me to identify his body. Joe and Joe Ann, his aunt and uncle, identified his body. They requested a chaplain to come and pray for me. I couldn't look at my child like that. On the way to the hospital, Joe said a police officer called and said "the report was wrong; a man was moving someone, and it had something to do with the accident, and if the family doesn't say anything, nothing would be done about it." I was too crazy. I couldn't think clearly. Joe notified his father. I was feeling the extreme, devastating loss, and I was not in my right mind to contact anyone.

My son was killed on August 31, 2011. My youngest daughter, Sheri was preparing to start her first year of college. My son, Paul, was in school in Carbondale, Illinois, and he came up for the funeral. My oldest daughter Jackie and my grandson came to the funeral. Art's father made the funeral arrangements for our son. My mother and my oldest brother, Junior, came after I pleaded with them. The day after they arrived, when I went into the kitchen, my mother walked by and said softly, "you shouldn't mind that he's gone. He was just a lot of trouble." I'm only saying this because my mother has passed. I was too grief stricken to respond to my mother. I'm just sharing my pain. We made it through the funeral, which was September 10, 2001.

The next day was September 11, 2001.

Sheri and her father had taken her things to her school, this was her first year of college, and she returned for the funeral. She was resting her head in my lap, while her father tried to secure her flight back to school. A friend called me about some business, and she explained something had happened and there were no flights. She asked, "are you listening to the news? No one can get a flight." I turned on the television, and I lost it.

I went into shock!

Upon receiving the accident report from the police, I almost went crazy. It said my son was running down the sidewalk, ran between parked cars, and ran into the side of an eighteen-wheeler. That statement was insanity for me because I drove an eighteen-wheeler, and there's no way he could run into the side of a truck. Sheri and I went to Lincoln Park, where my son was killed, to ask questions. We met a woman, who had retired from the State's Attorney's office. She asked questions for me in the community. She said a neighbor, who was sitting on his porch, saw the whole thing. My son asked two Black men, who were apparently moving someone if they needed any help. My son had a tendency to be persistent, even with me. One of the men pulled a gun on him. he ran out into the street. Their truck was doubled-parked, so he ran in front of the parked truck and, at the same time, an eighteen wheeler was speeding in the same direction, so he didn't see my son and my son didn't see him. The police wrote a restricted report that only I could get, stating he had burglarized someone's home. The woman that gave me the information said there had not been a burglary and the police had made it up. We both concluded those men must have been police officers, as to why they covered it up. No lawyer would touch the case.

I went to the Police Operational standard and internal affairs to get at the truth. They didn't want to help me. A new police station had opened at that time. They had a ceremony, and the Chief of Police and the Mayor attended. I spoke to the Police Chief. I told him the police killed my son. I went to the Mayor and told him no one would help me.

I fell apart, but remembered what Christ had said: "I will show you the great things you will suffer for my namesake." he also said, "I will take out your stony heart and give you a heart of flesh." I lost my apartment: had to go to a shelter; I became so depressed I had to go to the hospital for treatment, all these things happen after the death of my son. However, the Lord said I had to forgive my former boss. I forgave and released him. I forgave my mother because she was sick. Before she died, I did all I could for my mother. I forgave the police officer and the young truck driver that had just turned twenty one years old two months prior, for accidentally killing my son. As a result, the Lord gave me an apartment, with no money, companionship, and hope. He taught me not to be so quick to judge. I couldn't get work. I had to get food stamps and live in a shelter. You never know what devastating things are going on in a person's life. We need to love them where they are.

The Lord said the devil thought if he killed my son, I would stop serving the Lord. Well, no matter what!

"Though He slay me, yet will I trust Him!" (NKJV)

My maiden name is Cynthia Dobbins; I was born in an all black town, Mound Bayou, MS on January 2, 1950. My birth was at the beginning of the year; at the beginning of the Civil Rights Movement. I believe Jesus has appointed me for such a time as this to continue with the Civil Rights movement. There is still much to be done in the way of healing for this nation. More than anything this country needs to be healed from the ramifications of its past. "END RACISM NOW!"

≫ YOLANDA DUPREE ≪

A Creative Life

A Creative Life

"*I* was rushing out the house for the biggest day of my life, but I couldn't remember where I had put my phone. Rushing wasn't new for me, but today wasn't the day to be late. After all, you don't get to have lunch with the coolest President and his family every day. I took one last look at myself in the mirror to make sure I'd chosen the right dress and accessories. I also checked my makeup. It was important that I looked my best and I wanted to make a great impression.

"Once I got in the taxi and told the driver that our destination was The White House, I decided to Google pictures of place settings (oh, I found my phone on the bathroom counter next to my makeup) because I didn't want to make a fool of myself by using the wrong fork at the wrong time with the wrong course. After viewing a few pictures, I decided that I would watch the person that would be seated next to me at lunch, because I couldn't concentrate enough to remember anything. Excited was an understatement and I was doing everything I knew to do so I wouldn't have sweaty hands for my most memorable handshake.

"Oh, let me tell you how I was chosen for such a special event. I simply wrote a letter and asked if I could have lunch with the first family and they wrote me back and said yes. Yep, just like that! Well… actually, they were already planning a farewell luncheon so I was added to the guest list."

"Claire, why do you tell these crazy stories? Where do you get them from? Sweetheart, I need you to focus on your treatments and stop wasting your energy by making up these crazy stories. The more you talk, the more stress you put on your lungs." Olivia, Claire's mother, was frustrated.

"Okay, but can I tell you what we had for lunch and then I'll rest? Momma, the room was breathtaking and the food was perfectly placed on the plates like artwork. We had curry chicken salad, veggie pasta, shrimp cocktail, grilled pork loin with sautéed apples, grilled and steamed veggies, and fresh yeast rolls. There were plenty of fruit and appetizers. Mom, everything was delicious!"

"Okay, great! I'm glad you enjoyed yourself. Now, can we get back to reality?" asked an impatient Olivia.

"This is *my* reality." Claire continued talking to herself about the luncheon.

Feeling defeated, Olivia walked out of the room. She stood in the middle of the hall and stared at nothing. Doctors were being paged over the intercom, patients were being transported for tests, and family members rushed to find the rooms of their loved ones. Olivia just stood there, captive to the thoughts running rampant through her mind.

"Excuse me, ma'am, but can I help you? Is everything okay?" The voice came from a lady across the hall at the nurse's station that was small in stature, but her voice claimed your attention immediately. She walked around the desk toward Olivia.

"No, no thank you. I'm okay...I think," Olivia replied.

"What can I do to help you? Do you need anything?" Nurse Johnson had seen this look on the faces of far too many parents and it was the "break point look" that she recognized on Olivia.

"Well, actually, yes there is. My daughter is going to die if her treatments don't start to work soon. I'm trying to get her to focus, but all she wants to talk about are her make believe stories, stories about things she'll never actually do or accomplish. She's too young for her life to be stolen by an unexplainable birth defect. She's been through so many treatments," Olivia paused. As defeated tears rolled down her face, Olivia continued, "I'm trying to stay positive, but I fear my child has given up. It seems as if she has stopped fighting."

With as much compassion as she could express, Nurse Johnson said, "Ms. Olivia, I'm so sorry. Maybe I should call for the Chaplain to come pay you a visit. Will that be okay?"

"Yes, that would be great. I think that it's time for me to accept what's happening." Olivia wiped her tears. "I need some fresh air and maybe some coffee."

One hour later, Olivia was walking toward the room and could hear Claire laughing and another voice speaking from inside the room. To her surprise, it was Ms. Anderson from The Spring Forward Academy for Disabled Students.

"Oh my goodness, this is an awesome surprise! How did you know we were here?" Olivia asked, walking in the room.

"I didn't...I'm the Chaplain on duty today." The women embraced in a hug that to Olivia seemed awkward, but in a good way. It was as if Ms. Anderson, whom she hadn't seen in three years, connected with her and relieved all her stress and anxiety.

Ms. Anderson gave her a soft pat on the back, let her hand fall to meet Olivia's hand, and gave it a slight squeeze.

"So, how are you holding up? Is there anything I can do for you or anyone you would like for me to call?" asked Ms. Anderson.

Well, we're doing okay. Claire has been talking all day, but I told her that she needs to rest. She—"

Cutting her off, Ms. Anderson said, "Yes, she was telling me about her visit to the White House and, according to Claire, it was absolutely fabulous!" Although Ms. Anderson was talking to Olivia, she was looking at Claire as if they had a secret, an unspoken connection.

Olivia released Mrs. Anderson's hand and walked over to the table next to the bed to sit her coffee down. Now, the two women stood on opposite sides of Claire's bed.

"Ms. Anderson, may I ask you something?" Olivia asked, but didn't wait for a response before continuing. "When Claire attended Spring Forward Academy, I would come to pick her up, you would tell her goodbye and then whisper something in her ear. I asked Claire on several occasions to tell me your big secret, but she would just mumble something about creating living dreams or letting her mind be her playground. I never really understood what she meant by that. Can you explain it to me, please? Because not too long after we left the school, she started telling these stories…fantasies, make-believe stories of all kinds of things and adventures. These were things she would never be able to do, but she really believed they were true."

Ms. Anderson looked at Olivia for a moment and then down at Claire. As she took a deep breath and began to talk, a tear slowly rolled down her cheek and she smiled as if she was satisfied with herself.

She was just about to explain, but Claire cleared her throat and said, "Momma, Ms. Anderson was simply encouraging me to live and live now. To create in my mind all of the things I couldn't physically do, but could experience them fully with my imagination. By creatively living my dreams, in my short time on God's green earth, I've lived more than most people three times my age. Mom, I started living my wildest dreams. When I was twelve, I remember the doctors telling you I wouldn't live past fifteen years of age. Well, now I'm nineteen years old and I have lived a very full and exciting life. Let me share some of it with you."

Olivia sat on the side of the bed and motioned for Ms. Anderson to sit on the other side of the bed. Claire reached for both of their hands and shared…

"I've been many places and never left the room. I would close my eyes and see myself in auditoriums, standing before thousands of people who came to hear my story of triumph and perseverance…standing there with positivity flowing from my lips to every heart open to receive. I watched movies and placed myself as the leading actress with an Oscar-winning performance. I've been in three motion movies, one horror show, and five romantic movies because I have so much love to give. I've swam with dolphins, been zip lining, and had lunch with our 44th President. I've stomped the runway in a couture fashion show for renowned designer, Yoli, of Pixibags by Yoli. I've danced on stages across the world, scored winning goals in soccer and commentated in the press box for the Super Bowl. I've helped tear down walls that promote hate and discrimination and that's not all. I sang the national anthem better than Whitney Houston at our Relay for Life event… Okay, I'm stretching it a bit because no one has sung it better than her."

Olivia and Ms. Anderson laughed for a moment.

"Oh yeah, let me tell you this!" Claire's eyes lit up with excitement as she continued with her stories. "I also visited the National Museum of African American History and Culture. As I walked through the halls, I heard our pioneers and heroes speaking their truths to me, but ironically, I also heard them urging me to share my truth. My truth is that although this physical shell of mine is dying, my spirit is living in full color. My organs are slowly losing their functions, but my imagination is running faster than ever, but I won't be here much longer."

Olivia looked up at Ms. Anderson and gasped, while tears streamed down her face.

Claire kept talking. "Momma, I've won eating contests and fallen in love with the man of my dreams. He and I shared our love for each other on our wedding night in an ocean-view cabana on a private patio under the stars of the pacific. And now, right now, Momma…" Claire's breathing began to really slow down and was more labored.

Olivia asked, "What is it, Claire? What's happening?"

Claire took a deep breath, smiled, and said, "I'm giving birth to your granddaughter. She's beautiful! Momma, I'm so tired."

"All right, Claire, maybe you should stop talking now." Olivia turned to Ms. Anderson and said, "We should go get someone. She's not breathing well and looks a little pale. I'm scared."

"Momma, don't be scared, I'm fine.

Can I have my gift now, Momma?" Claire was staring across the room.

"What gift?" asked Olivia.

"There's a man standing in the corner of the room with a beautiful box. He's been here all day. He says my wings are in the box. If I take the wings, then I can fly. Momma, that's the one thing I've never experienced and wow, they're beautiful, multicolored sparkling wings! Can I have my wings now, Momma?"

Olivia didn't say anything for a few moments because she knew what was happening. Through her tears, she said, "It has been my pleasure being your mother and I'm so glad you had Ms. Anderson to help you live your creative dreams. And I'm going to miss you so much, more than you will ever know." She paused and took what seemed to be an eternity, but finally said, "Yes, my Dear Sweet Claire, go get your wings." She leaned over, kissed her forehead, and stayed there until Claire took her final breath.

Ms. Anderson decided to leave and gave Olivia a few moments alone with Claire, but just before she walked out the room, she turned around and said, "This was a beautiful exchange. Have you ever heard of the scripture that says, 'Some have entertained angels unawares?' You gave Claire the chance to live by giving birth to her, even though it wasn't the life you wanted for her. Olivia, I hope you realize the gift Claire has now given you. She has left you with the gift of nothing is impossible. The gift of living life through your imagination and then making it manifest in reality. Claire's imagination was her reality, but you can create *your* reality through your imagination."

Olivia wiped her tears. "The funny thing is, I didn't want to hear her stories because they reminded me of things I wanted to do, but fear and other people's opinions would stop me every time."

"Olivia, the world is your playground. You are very special and must have something remarkably important to do because God sent you an angel. He sent you, you! You needed to see the possibilities of life, an exceeding abundantly, more life. You will always miss Claire, but you must not get stuck in your grief. Just keep moving forward and please, take care of yourself." Ms. Anderson smiled and left the room.

One week after Claire's homegoing service, Olivia returned to the hospital to see Ms. Anderson to give her a thank you card, but was told that no one by that name or description had ever worked there as a Chaplain.

Yolanda Dupree

Yolanda attended Arnold International University of Cosmetology and received her Master Cosmetologist license from the State of Georgia in 1990. She also received her certification as a Christian Life Coach from New Life Coach Inc. in 2010. Yolanda is President of Dupree Empowerment Group Inc., a 501c3 nonprofit group whose mission is to support the community and strengthen families through love, motivation and education. She is a motivational speaker and author of 3 books: To God Be the Glory, Countdown to Your Last 90 Days and Five Key Components to Finding Your Purpose.

With that being said, Yolanda loves people, loves to eat, laugh, and create. She isn't afraid to cry or tell it like it is and most importantly, she believes that the impossible is possible. Yolanda and Michael have been married for 22 years and have four beautiful children, Xavier, Jada, Kayla, and Jonathan.

⫷ BETTY EFEMINI ⫸

Arise and Fulfill Your Potential

Arise and Fulfill Your Potential

I have never considered myself a creative person or artist in any way. Although, I do believe we are born with skills and talents that lay dormant for years because we do not realize we have them, which also means we aren't tapping into them, developing them or nurturing them.

A skill is an ability to do an activity or a job.

A talent is a natural ability to be good at something without learning it.

I believe I am not creative and I do not have any creative or artistic skills, like other people, who were born with it. If you have this mind-set and believe that is true, then you will act on that belief. You perceive it to be true and believe it.

I have two left hands. I cannot create anything not even hem a skirt. I would not wear it again, or take to be dry-cleaned sewing is just not me.

When I was ten years old, I learnt how to crochet and now I cannot even remember how to do it.

When I was pregnant with my first daughter, my friend taught me to knit. I really enjoyed knitting baby booties, hats, and cardigans. I even knitted a jumper and a cardigan for myself. Then, I stopped.

My eldest sister came from Nigeria and taught me how to braid hair. I enjoyed that and got many customers. I stopped because my friends would always visit me with a pack of hair and get their hair done free. After a while, I told them I forgot how to braid because I had not done it for a while.

I am not a creative person is what my mind keeps telling me.

I went to evening classes and learnt how to do make-up, and I really enjoyed it. I was going to be a makeup artist. I took three courses, developed my portfolio, and passed all my assignments. I was good at it. I then learnt manicures, nail art, and acrylic (fake) nails. I passed those courses, too.

I went for a job has a makeup artist, but I had made up my mind before I got there that I would fail. I was terribly afraid. I was in a big room with other makeup artists and their models. I spent a lot of time looking at what they were doing. How could I compete with them? I wondered why I would come there only to embarrass myself. This was pre-Internet when there were only books, and no makeup tutorials on YouTube or pictures on Google or any kind of social media to help you. I did not feel good about myself; my confidence level was at zero. I made up my model to the best of my ability. She told me she really liked what I had done. I thought she was just saying that to make me feel good. I was happy when it was over. While leaving the venue, I thought, *Thank God that is all over.* There was no way they would call me back, after all I had already convinced myself that I had done a rubbish job and all the others were better than me.

I received a call from the company and they liked my work, and wanted me to work with them and when work becomes available they would call me. I held the phone, thinking, *Maybe they called the wrong person. They cannot be talking about me. After all, my makeup skills are not that good.* Still, I had convinced myself that I was not a creative person.

MAC Cosmetics even offered me a job as a Make-up Artist in central London, working on weekends. I declined the job because I had to go to church on Sundays, which was true, but I was scared I would fail and I really was not that good. Yes, I could have taken the job and changed the shift for another day other than Sunday.

I continued with makeup because I enjoyed transforming faces with my Makeup skills. I did beauty pageants and photo shoots for free. I was also hired to do bridal makeup. I must have done a good job, because they actually paid me for it.

Yet, still, *I am not a creative person* was a permanent thought in my mind.

I pushed creative skills and talent thinking out of my mind. I decided to stick to what I was good at—a general job that would earn me money.

I had many jobs: cleaner, catering assistant, dinner lady, waitress, receptionist, administrative, customer service, sales assistant; after all, I did leave school with no qualifications. School was a fun place to go and an outlet for me. College was even better; it was all fun for me. I remember the older learners telling my friends and me to be quiet because we were always talking and laughing in class. I used to think, *What is wrong with them old people, aren't they enjoying the fun?* After all, I came to college to socialize and hang out with my girls. Not to learn that college was an extension of school. I was not in college to learn. I got grade G, which is the equivalent to zero, and the rest were unclassified, but back then you could get a job with no qualifications or experience. As long as you were willing you would get hired. Not all the stiff competition we see today for the most basic job.

I got a job in the local government and I worked there for ten years—first as a Typist in the legal department, then in the Housing Office as an Admin Officer, and then in the community as an Administrative Assistant in an Older People's Project. I enjoyed working at the Local Council, it was fun. I looked forward to going to work. I worked hard I enjoyed going to lunch for two hours and getting back to my desk, and nobody asked me any questions. Once I left after lunch and never came back. I was drinking in the pub and got drunk. I enjoyed going to the social club every Friday without fail after work, and coming home at midnight. I was set for life; I thought I could work there forever.

Until one day we were called to a meeting. We had no idea what the meeting was about. We found out that our department was deleting four hundred people. I saw people crying; some said they would refuse to leave. I thought it was funny; after all, I was still young—thirty years old with no mortgage. I thought, *If there is no job, what am I supposed to do?* I thought I would look for another job and if I could not find one, I would go on welfare—at least my rent would be paid and I would get money to maintain my two children and me. After all, I had been unemployed before and I did not die. I survived and had gotten my current job, which was now gone. I had a meeting with the Director of Social Services and the Human Resources Manager who asked me what I was going to do. I was not really sure, but I decided it was time to use my brain; I had one qualification since leaving school. I was going to be a mature student and go to university. They helped me find out information about enrolling in courses, which I really appreciated.

Seriously, upon reflection, I realized I was immature about the day I got made redundant after ten years of working. I understand that those people who were angry and upset were more mature and responsible than me; that their jobs were their source of income and they had just lost it, which is why they were so upset.

Fast forward, I am now a single parent with two children doing an HND in Business and Finance. This was very hard for me; I had never studied like this before, and now I was serious. When I saw all the young people messing about, I remembered how I was in college. There was no Internet then, only books in the library and when you got to the particular page where you would get the information it was ripped out. It was hard work; I don't think I enjoyed it. I just wanted to pass. I passed the first year exams. In the second year of the course, I got pregnant, but I continued to do the course. I was scheduled to take the exams in June, but I went into labor the day of the first exam so I missed out on taking the exams. I retook the exams three months, later did the assignments while breast-feeding my son and passed with flying colors. My tutors were surprised how well I had done. I was now focused.

I earned an HND in Business and Finance. I was proud of myself. I had a brain after all.

I went on to do my degree in Business and Marketing. I was also one of the eldest people in the class

I did not have a social life; it was all church, course work, and exams. The younger people would ask me how I managed with three children and studying. I told them I pray to God daily for Him to help me with my work. They believe me after all it was the grace of God to study and pass this course.

It wasn't easy to pass. I had done well in my assignments and exams, but I nearly failed because my dissertation was scrap and I knew it was, but I was physically and mentally tired by then. That was the best I could do. I did pass and got my degree in

Business and Marketing. I was very proud of myself; not only did I have a brain, it was also working. I had letters after my name.

I would often show my kids my graduation picture and I told them that their picture would be hanging next to mind one day. At least when I filled out application forms now the qualification page was no longer blank.

Now it was time to get a job. I thought because I had a degree I could get a job. I was surprised to learn that since I left school sixteen years ago, things had changed. It was not that easy to get a job. You need qualifications, skills and experience. It was competitive. I decided I wanted to become an IT Help Desk Support Engineer. I went to see my advisor at the job centre who told me I should forget that idea, that I would be better off being a secretary. I told him no way. I did not go to university to be a secretary. After much disagreement and many appointments, he agreed to fund training so I could become an IT Engineer. This experience reminded me when I was at school and the career advisor told me I should work in a shop. I told her no, I was going to work in an office. She looked at me as if I'd lost my mind. In those days, in the '70s, uneducated girls were advised to work in a shop or a factory when they left school; no way could they go to college as that was like a camel entering the eye of a needle.

After fighting so hard to get funding to take the Microsoft Certified Solutions Expert exams, I changed my mind for a career in IT. After I got a job as IT Second Line Support Engineer, I was the only woman among men.

The conversations those guys used to have were out of order and they always forgot I was there, as they expressed all kinds of rude jokes. Then they would look and me a say, "Sorry." Or I would go to fix a computer and they would ask me if I needed any help. Plus the hours were family unfriendly, definitely not for a woman with children. I thought this was nonsense. Sometimes all that glitters is not gold. I did not want to be an IT Engineer anymore.

So now what I was going to do? My dream career had not worked out so I had to go back to the drawing board. I needed a career that would fit around by children, so I decided to become a teacher.

That meant going back to University. I knew I was capable of passing any course now. So I enrolled in a Post Graduate Teacher Training for two years and worked as a part time lecturer in various colleges. At one stage, I had four different jobs.

Eventually, three years after my degree and during my teaching training, I got a full time job teaching at a local college, where I really enjoyed working. I met many wonderful people. I enjoyed teaching adults who had a second chance at education and learning new skills. No one is too old to learn.

My oldest student was a ninety-one-year-old deaf man who wanted to learn how to use the computer to communicate with his family via Skype in Australia

I finished Teacher Training when I was thirty-eight years old. In the United Kingdom, we can retire at sixty-five years old, so there is plenty of time, but sadly many people over fifty years old find it hard to gain employment and the job market is very competitive. Sadly, after twelve years of working at the college I got made redundant a few weeks before my fiftieth birthday. I was happy while I was at the college.

While working at the college trained to be a health promoter because my best friend died of a heart attack. She had high blood pressure and was diabetic. I remember telling her, "Let's go to the gym," but she was just unmotivated. The last day she left a message on my phone was the night she died. I was so sad. I got a part time job has a health promoter in a local gym and I empowered people about their health and wellness. I always tell clients that their health is their wealth, and they cannot buy their health back with money.

Now I am educated. I understood the importance of being educated. I continued to learn new skills and took creative skills courses. I learnt how to make jewellery, flower arranging and balloon making. I also taught myself how to use a computerized embroidery machine. Now I have creative skills as well. I have good range of skills and experience and my creative skills has been ignited. I went on to school of social entrepreneurs and Unltd. These organizations help and support individuals to become social entrepreneurs, helping them to establish a social project which solves a social issue. Creative people are less likely to be supported or taken serious compared to those who have academic skills I founded a creative crafts training and enterprise project that teaches people in the community creative and craft skills. I started teaching machine embroidery, a skill I taught myself. I have ignited my passion of teaching and creativity and working in the local community. I now work with other creative artists who have a skill and want to teach that skill. I found a whole community of people who were creative artists that had excellent skills and created amazing items. I encouraged them to join the project and teach their skills. To date, there is a Fashion Designer, a Knitting Artist, Jeweller, an Embroidery Artist and Upholstery Designer—all of whom are self-taught and come from different career backgrounds. I have now set up the creative crafts boutique, which is a creative craft and enterprise program.

We share our skills and talents; we connect, create, and sell. We bring people together to learn a creative skill and we love doing it. We work with a wide range of people from the elderly, people with mental health problems, disabled and children.

Many of our clients enjoy the courses. Apart from creativity, we are friendly and very social. Our journey has been very exciting and amazing. We are in demand; we have been asked to work with many groups in the community and have been offered the opportunity to work in Nigeria, Uganda and Ghana. We want to set up a craft co-operative in the future, but we need funds and need to train more tutors.

I no longer hear that voice in my head telling me I am not creative and not good enough. You can do anything you want to do. You just have to make up your mind that you can and want to do it, and the rest is history. Don't bury your skills and talents they have no use in the cemetery. Use them to help empower and inspire others the world is waiting to hear about you.

"May all that has been reduced to noise in you
become music again" - Unknown

Not only can God grant you the desire of your heart, He will also give you opportunities to make them come to pass.

Betty B Efemini is passionate about people being empowered, motivated and living a life of destiny and purpose and hope. Betty functioned in many roles. Volunteer Chaplin, Missionary, Social Entrepreneur Health and Career Coach, Lecturer, IT Trainer and Embroidery Artist and founder of Holistic Well Women and the Creative Craft Boutique a non for profit organisation set up to promote

Betty Efemini

and provide creative craft, enterprise and business empowerment support, and Health and Well being and educational activities in her local community. Betty resides in London United Kingdom with her family.

Spared for God's Purpose

Spared for God's Purpose

*"You intended to harm me, but God intended it
for good to accomplish what is now being done, the
saving of many lives."*
— Genesis 50:20 (NIV)

At age four, while crossing the street in front of my house, I was struck by a hit and run drunken driver. A traumatic brain injury left my brain lying on the sidewalk. Doctors told my parents I wouldn't survive, and if I did, I would be a vegetable. My praying mother, grandfather, and aunts rushed to my bedside. They anointed me with oil and believed God for my healing. I have spent my entire life listening to them testify about how God brought me out of the coma in three days and how I *walked* out of the hospital in thirteen days. They also emphasized how I always excelled in school, and how God was to be glorified.

At age twenty, I was being treated for Ulcerative Colitis and was given a sulfa-based medication. At that time, I did not know I had G6-PD Blood Deficiency. As a result, I spent three weeks in the hospital with a mild case of Stevens-Johnson Syndrome (SDS). It began with flu-like symptoms, followed by a painful red or purplish rash over my body that spread and blistered. The entire top layer of my affected skin died and had shed once healing began. The enemy meant it for evil to take my life, but God meant it for good.

Five years earlier, during a fight with one of my siblings, I received second-degree burns from hot coffee that was tossed in my face and settled on my chest. By the time I reached the hospital, blisters covered my chest. The physician ripped off the blisters, bandaged me up, and sent me home. I lived with the physical scars on my chest for all those years, often wondering whether it would be repulsive to my future spouse. *But God!* During the Stevens-Johnson episode, when my skin shed, so did the physical scars from the burns.

Called For Such A Time As This

"For if you remain silent at this time, relief and deliverance for the Jews will arise from another place, but you and your father's family will perish. And who knows but that you have come to your royal position for such a time as this?"
—Esther 4:14 NIV

A calling is the gift and burden (the things that keep you up at night) that is colliding. Although it was difficult to share my story, my burden is to raise awareness, assist and help people see mental illness from a different point of view. God wants people to have faith and know that they can make it through the fog of mental illness to success. Many experts have said that many people have the gene of mental illness lying dormant in their brain; however, it often times is never ignited unless there is a traumatic event or traumatic brain injury that takes place in their lives. As people read this or my full story in *Faith Through The Fog*

To Success; when it is published, I pray their faith will grow in the realization that God is with us, knows our struggles, and can give us the stamina needed as we persevere. Believing that He alone can take what was meant for evil, and bless us to live a life that is full of purpose. We can live on purpose and be a demonstration of God's ability to turn our mess into a message. He never comforts us to be comfortable, but so we can comfort others.

"God, if it is in Your best interest to remove this suffering, please do so. But if it fulfills Your purpose, that's what I want, too."

I was forty when diagnosed with Bipolar Disorder II. The onset of the illness resulted from a car accident that my older sister and her boyfriend had on Christmas day when I was thirteen years old. Blocks from my oldest sister's apartment building, their car spun on the snowy road and wrapped around a utility pole. I sat in the emergency room and all the parents were in tears. Shortly after that, someone escorted his parents down the hallway to a place where his mother's screams seemed to engulf the hospital. The despair within her cry told me, without words, the accident had claimed her son's life. My sister's boyfriend was a man who I held dear to my heart and considered a big brother.

I was now experiencing my first major loss and hospitalization, as my sister lay comatose for nearly a month following that accident. My sister remained in the hospital for close to five months, but my mother had to return to work shortly after the accident. In those days, I was not of legal age to visit my sister. Every evening, I had a different story for my mother about how I evaded the security guards in order to visit with her and monitor her progress. All the photos of my sister's boyfriend were destroyed in an effort to protect her from this devastating loss once she regained consciousness. For reasons unknown to me, we never attended his funeral, which further impacted the loss since he was like a big brother to me. He made me laugh all the time and gave me my first amethyst birthstone ring. I genuinely admired them both as I often recollected the joy on their faces and the stunning fur jacket my sister wore when they journeyed out the afternoon of the accident. My sister was hurt badly and she had a long road to recover from such a tragic accident.

I was diagnosed after a crisis that took place during daylight savings time in the spring, which causes an imbalance in people with Bipolar Disorder. That spring, I began waking up and crying for no reason every morning. I loved my job, but was having a difficult time getting ready to venture into work for weeks. One morning, I was speaking to my friend, Jamel, who, at that point, had known me for thirteen years, rocked my two babies, and provided me with shelter during my period of homelessness. Prior to our meeting, she had a friend who had Bipolar Disorder and stated that my symptoms sounded similar, so I should be evaluated. I also shared it with my other friend, Trilbie, who had known me for nine years. We met rocking our daughters, Alexandria and Jélissa, in the lobby of church when there was no nursery. Trilbie had a great deal of knowledge and experience with the disorder, too. She had witnessed friends and their families endure some debilitating and fatal outcomes as a result. She concurred with Jamel's advice to seek professional help since this crying episode had lasted for more than a month.

I had experienced bouts of severe depression throughout my life, beginning at age thirteen. I described this life as being one that mimics the song's lyrics, "The tears of a clown, when there's no one around." I say this because I would make every effort to be happy and make others happy, but I would often go in private places and cry for hours. I often contemplated suicide and proceeded to cut at my wrists a few times. I do realize now that the times I cut at my wrists, I felt like I just wanted to die. I always thought about how much pain that would cause my parents and others in my life if I ended it, so I just wanted someone to acknowledge my state and help me feel better. Afterwards, I would feel so embarrassed, so I hid my wrists from them until the scars faded.

For years, I battled with financial troubles and was never able to save or finish things I started because of mood swings, mania, and depression. I often went for days without sleep, and then would eventually encounter crashing. When the cycle of crashing happens, I would become extremely depressed and could not function. Once diagnosed with Bipolar Disorder, I went to counseling and began the process of finding the right combination of medication. Medication management was difficult because I have a high sensitivity to medications. Because I had spent many years staying up late at night obsessed with fixing the house when I was frustrated and unable to fix other things in my life, I had to learn how to sleep again. I wanted desperately to fix my marriage and finances, but didn't realize that my difficulty applying God's Word to those areas was rooted in this illness. When manic, I would stay up shopping online and obsessively reading product reviews, redecorating, or emailing friends. When I began to embrace my healing process, I soon learned that as great of a person my husband was, he was not equipped or willing to handle the diagnosis. This was a painful awakening as it was at a time when I was struggling with finding the right medications and addressing some painful issues in counseling. I desperately wanted my life partner to understand and give me his full support;

however, my attempt at normalcy created an even greater gap in my marriage. Adding to the problems we faced because of the mania, were the constant financial hardships. His overspending was an attempt to feel better while coping with life's challenges and his anger; however, it also added to my stress and further impacted my illness.

My life partner was now in the grieving process because he had lost the infallible wife he envisioned me to be. He became extremely antagonistic toward me because he fell in love, as did many others, with the manic woman who appeared to be accomplishing it all; thereby a glorified "cover girl," who covered it all from the bedroom to the boardroom. My husband was not willing to accept the mood swings for what they were, so he interpreted them as rejection.

For a long time, I would hurt my children because I would become angry and they couldn't understand why. This also happened a great deal when I was a teenager. While enjoying each other's company, an innocent joke would always end with me running upstairs in tears and sinking into a depression.

My daughter bore the brunt of most of my anger and mood swings because I did not enter treatment until she was nine years old. Although I continued to have these mood swings for years, prayer, medication, and treatment taught me how to handle them. I began to tell my children that whenever my mood changed, I was feeling overstimulated. They would step back and give me the space I needed for it to pass.

One of the greatest challenges for my children was seeing how angry I became toward my husband. They would hear the arguing, but I was the one throwing things and screaming. When it came time to separate, my daughter remained with her father and my son moved out with me. My husband's contributions to the arguments were less obvious, and therefore undetected by the children. Because my daughter saw my behavior and experienced it firsthand, the separation was, in her perspective, entirely my fault. After a year of living on my own in a nontoxic environment, they began to see the manageability of the illness and the kind characteristics that God had developed outside of the illness.

> *"Father I thank You that even when we fall short as parents You are a father to the fatherless and a mother to the motherless. I thank You that You love our children and have plans to prosper them in spite of our afflictions. I pray that you continue to heal any brokenness and erase any trace of the wounds of childhood devastations in Jesus' name."*

In a recent conversation with a friend, whose mother suffered from paranoid schizophrenia, she shared that after her father passed away and she was no longer in a toxic relationship, her mother's illness became totally manageable. People with Bipolar and other mental illnesses can have successful marriages, but our marriage was extremely toxic; there were some deep-rooted issues in both of our personalities, thought processes and pasts that was not addressed before we came together. It is possible to have a healthy marriage in spite of mental illness, but marriage is hard and it takes a willing partner. That person must realize that this is a huge undertaking, so it is important to count the cost. You must seek God in this crucial decision that will greatly affect you, as well as impact family and friends who are intertwined in your lives.

When I was initially diagnosed, I thought I could share that information with everyone, but I quickly found, for various reasons, that it wasn't for everyone to know. As I matured in counseling,

I found the right combination of medications; slept more, lost weight, abandoned unhealthy relationships and established accountability partners. Those who were willing to accept it and help in my healing would question me when they realized I had been up sending emails to them throughout the night. I spend a great deal of time laughing because the Bible says that a merry heart is like medicine. I confess regularly as I take communion at home, that by God's stripes I was healed. I believe I am healed, although I continue to take medication and attend counseling because that is what God says in His Word. By spending as much time in the Word as possible and following my treatment plan, my moods are steadier than they have ever been before.

AND, I RISE

"The silver is mine and the gold is mine,' declares the Lord Almighty. 'The glory of this present house will be greater than the glory of the former house,' says the Lord Almighty. 'And in this place I will grant peace,' declares the Lord Almighty"
— (Haggai 2:8-9 NIV)

As previously stated, I left the home we purchased and I poured my love into, and my marriage of twenty-eight years because of the relational toxicity and verbal abuse. My daughter chose to stay, so my heart was terribly torn and saddened without her. For my own sanity, I left, but also to be an example to my children. I wanted them to know two things: if they become an abuser, the person will eventually get the courage to leave them; and if they are being abused, they can step out on faith and trust God's love to walk them into the abundant and healthy life that

He has for them. It has been five years, and since that time, I have faced many arduous situations that required me to have an insurmountable amount of faith in God. At times, I did not know how I would meet my financial obligations or avoid an irreversible mental collapse. There were instances when I was at the brink of disaster and losing my mind. Praise God for the ministry of Pastor Dharius and Shameka Daniels who God has used to show me the principles of what healthy relationships should look like, and how to live with purpose.

I've had the love of my children, friends, family, and church family to cover me. Time and care heals all wounds, and along with that support system, I am constantly stable. I continue counseling, take a minimal amount of medication and supplements, exercise regularly, and, above all, spend time daily with God in prayer and His Word. While it was grievous to walk away from a twenty-eight-year relationship I put all of my hopes and dreams in, the Word says that God will *"provide for those who grieve in Zion—to bestow on them a crown of beauty instead of ashes, the oil of joy instead of mourning, and a garment of praise instead of a spirit of despair. They will be called oaks of righteousness, a planting of the LORD FOR THE DISPLAY OF HIS SPLENDOR,"* (Isaiah 61:3 NIV). However, in order to get the beauty and praise, you have to embrace the lessons learned from the past, and surrender the ashes as well as the spirit of despair. The past was meant to learn from and not to live in. [16] *"This is what the LORD SAYS—HE WHO MADE A WAY THROUGH THE SEA, A PATH THROUGH THE MIGHTY WATERS,* [17] *who drew out the chariots and horses, the army and reinforcements together, and they lay there, never to rise again, extinguished, snuffed out like a wick:* [18] *"Forget the former things; do not dwell on the past.* [19] *See, I am doing a new thing! Now it springs up; do you not perceive it? I am making a way in the wilderness and streams in the wasteland,"* (Isaiah 43:16-19).

Something new means it hasn't been done before. I now have a new job and income that is double what I was making when I departed that abusive relationship. I prayed three years ago for God to double my income, but in the past two years, it was done in ways I would've never imagined. It was truly exceedingly abundantly above what i could ask. When you ask God for restoration and increase, leave the method up to Him. I have a brand new vehicle; and God also blessed me to purchase a two-bedroom condo. My daughter is happily married to a wonderful young man named Terrell and they are pregnant with a baby girl. My son is completing his final year of high school and he is in route to college. Don't let your mistakes, illness or anything from YESterday ruin your YES today. YES! No matter what you have walked through in the past, no matter the sadness, the loss, the failure, or oppression, with faith in God, YOU CAN RISE AGAIN, TOO.

Lisa Frank is the founder of Lisa Frank's Empowerment Services. She has a Bachelor's Degree in Theology from The United Bible College & Seminary of Orlando, Florida. She is a Certified Life Coach and Motivational Speaker with a crisis, grief, and loss niche. She volunteers yearly at Camp Erin Philadelphia for grieving children who have experienced significant losses. Lisa has worked in banking for thirteen years; been an addictions counselor for eighteen years; nutrition counselor for many years, and has worked as a Home Health Aide. The counseling field has exposed her to a diversity of populations with people suffering from many forms of mental illness.

Her mental health experience began in a residential halfway house for women and children recovering from drug and alcohol addictions; and continued at such venues as methadone clinics, correctional facilities, family practices, and other rehabilitation centers. She has counseled and educated thousands of people, primarily women, through life's challenges. She is culturally sensitive and has studied abroad for extended periods in Madrid, Spain and San Jose, Costa Rica. She also completed a minor in Communications Disorders at The College of New Jersey. She obtained both a Clinical Medical Assistant and Phlebotomy certification that has led to her current work in the healthcare field. Her primary joy and calling in life is being a mother to her daughter Jélissa and son Oscar. To reach out to me, email: coachlisafrankspeaks@gmail.com.

❋ ANGELA PATTERSON ❋

I Remember Mommy

I Remember Mommy

*S*itting in my apartment, in my favorite chair, wrapped in my chenille purple throw, drinking my favorite herbal chamomile tea, I gaze out the large glass sliding door from the living room onto my balcony, watching the colorful leaves fall from the trees. It amazes me how beautiful nature is, seeing God's hand in everything.

Three days before Thanksgiving, thirty-two years ago in 1984, I was nineteen years old at the time.

I remember my mother, Lorraine Dews Patterson, a beautiful, light brown-skinned, petite woman with the biggest chubby cheeks and small brown freckles. When she smiled, her face lit up the room. You couldn't help but smile with her and at her because her cheeks would become more inflated the more she smiled. I would try to see how far she could spread the freckles on her face.

My mother, or Mommy as her five children affectionately called her, loved to sing or hum gospel songs. Lord knows she would be out of tune, humming away to a Mahalia Jackson gospel. Couldn't she hear herself? I can honestly say I have definitely inherited her singing challenge.

She taught us to love and revere the Lord. As children, she read Bible stories to us and, of course, every Sunday we attended Ebenezer Baptist Church in Orange, New Jersey. Reverend

79

Blossom would whoop and holler, energizing his flock to turn from their wicked ways and accept salvation.

After service, my twin brother Anthony and I used to play church, mimicking Reverend Blossom until we were almost filled with the Holy Ghost or caught by Mommy.

I laugh at how we tried to dance to one of Andre Crouch's popular church songs we would be yelled at about how we were disrespectful dancing and snapping our fingers to the Lord's music. How ironic is that? Now we are dancing and shouting to music from Kirk Franklin, Hezekiah Walker and Tasha Cobbs. Wow how times have surely changed.

Mommy was the original Martha Stewart, using all the skills her mother taught her. She made all our meals from scratch, including homemade desserts, keeping her most treasured recipes alphabetically in her yellow Betty Crocker recipe box she kept on the kitchen counter next to her metal canisters of flour and sugar. She would make our favorite meal for each of our birthdays and, of course, bake our desired multi-tiered cake, topped with the appropriate amount of candles that represented our new age.

Not only was she a great baker and cook, she also was a seamstress and sewed our clothing.

As much as she loved her children, she loved her husband, Phillip Collin Patterson, more. They would openly express their love for one another with sweet kisses, lovingly teasing each other while dancing to beautiful Motown love songs. Watching their love grow deeper even after having five children together, I knew this was what I wanted in my future marriage.

At twelve years old, my idyllic childhood was coming to an abrupt end. Mommy was diagnosed with breast cancer. I remember the fear and sadness in her eyes, how she always seemed to put up a brave front even after being physically ill or lacking energy. Still not knowing her diagnosis, but feeling as if something wasn't quite right, I wanted to help her. I wanted her to feel better.

One day after school, Mommy had prepared our usual snack of homemade baked cookies and a glass of milk. This time was different because she actually sat down at the kitchen table with us. I immediately knew something was wrong, as she began the conversation with the dreaded words, "There is nothing to worry about, I will be fine." Even at twelve, I knew when an adult started a conversation like that it most likely was not good news. She told us she was diagnosed with breast cancer, but she would be all right and not to worry. I had no idea what a mastectomy was. She then began to explain that the doctors were going to remove her breast and that she would be in the hospital for two weeks. I could see the pain in her eyes as she was telling her youngest babies her diagnosis.

It was evident she was keeping it together for our sakes and did not break down crying in front of us. She cleared her voice and her tone changed; she was now very serious, saying we needed to help out more around the house until she returned from the hospital. She reassured us that nothing was going to change and our routine would remain the same. I wanted to believe her, but deep down inside I knew this was the beginning of the end. I think Anthony was in shock because he never once moved or said a word, he just continued eating his cookies and looking down at the plate. I felt tears streaming down my cheeks. I reached over to her and hugged her so tightly, never wanting to let go. If only I could hug that cancer out of her. I grew up this day.

Mommy had the mastectomy and after feeling like an eternity, she returned home. While she was recovering from surgery, she also went through her chemotherapy treatments. This treatment took a toll on her small frame; she looked thin and frail.

When she returned home from the hospital, I helped her settle in for the evening, while Dad prepared dinner. Mommy handed me her hairbrush and asked me to brush her hair, as I always had done. When I brushed her hair, clumps of hair were in the brush. I stopped brushing and didn't know how to tell her that her beautiful soft black wavy hair was coming out in clumps. She reached over my shoulder, grabbed the brush out of my hand, and saw for herself. I saw one tear fall down the side of her cheek. She wiped her face and told me to look on her bureau and grab the scissors. I immediately did as she requested, not fully understanding what she wanted with the scissors. I grabbed the scissors and being very careful not to drop it, I tried to hand it over to her when she touched my hand and told me to cut off the rest of her hair. I knew I needed to be strong for her. Without saying a word, I began cutting her hair. I was determined that I was not going to cry because she needed my strength; she needed to know I agreed with her taking control over how she was going to lose her hair. At that moment, I was never more proud of her. She then declared, with tears in her eyes and a smile on her face, that she needed a wig since she no longer had hair. I nervously agreed and let out a small giggle. This was the first time I truly saw her being so vulnerable; she looked defeated.

It was the seventh year now and her treatments were getting more aggressive, alternating between chemotherapy and radiation. Her physical appearance was drastically changing; she still was a beautiful woman, but now extremely thin. She was weak and always tired. She spent most of the day in her bedroom. Her body was betraying her, but her mind was still sharp.

By now, I was nineteen in my second year of college and commuting. I hated having to spend time away from her. If it were up to me, I would have spent every waking moment with her, lying next to her in bed, watching soap operas and game shows, but she would not hear of that. So, the time we had together was more precious than ever. I would climb in the bed with her and just talk. We talked about her childhood, how she met Dad, my future career goals and then, without notice, she would discuss her wishes about funeral arrangements. I understood Dad probably didn't want to hear such talk of gloom and doom. I knew how strong their love was and he couldn't imagine his life without her.

She could not control her health, but she would have a say on how she would be buried. Because we were so much alike, Mommy knew I would respect and honor her wishes.

I instantly knew Mommy had made peace with dying. I overheard her conversation with Dad, one evening. She said her prayer was to live long enough to see her babies graduate from high school. God had answered her prayer so now she was ready to go home.

It was November 1984 when Dad drove Mommy to the hospital for a scheduled inpatient chemotherapy round. As he was pulling out of the driveway, she told him, "This is the last time I will see this house." He, being a great supportive husband, reassured her she would be back after the treatments as she has previously done. She didn't say another word, as he drove to the hospital in silence.

Early the next morning before my classes, Dad drove me to the hospital to see Mommy. He was going to return in an hour to pick me up so I could attend class. The moment I entered the room, I felt something was wrong. She looked so small lying in that hospital bed. She looked tired, not sleepy, but just worn out. The only food she could digest was pureed and she was even too weak to feed herself. I sat on the edge of her bed and attempted to feed her. She made such a face and jokingly told me to eat it. I made a similar face and shook my head, not opening my mouth for fear she would shove the spoon of nastiness in my mouth.

She pushed back the food tray and moved the covers on her bed, without uttering a word. That was my cue to get in the bed with her. I took my sneakers off and gently lay next to her. I felt the warmness of her body. I laid my head on her shoulder and just wanted to cry. It felt like goodbye.

After what appeared to be an eternity, Mommy began speaking. I was listening to every word she spoke, trying to put the sound of her voice within the memory of my heart and brain. I never wanted to forget how she sounded. Her tone was soft with loving care that only a mother who was dying could muster. She had a look in her eyes that I had never seen before. Her eyes were saying to my spirit that she would be all right; she was going home with the Lord. At this time in my life, I had not given my life to the Lord, but God showed me grace and mercy by allowing me to see Him in her eyes.

Dad returned to take me to class. He asked if I was ready to leave, and Mommy, with might and strength, said, "No, stay here." He looked at me so helpless with tears in his eyes, almost begging me to stay. Little did he know, I didn't want to leave. I softly said, "Yes," to Mommy. He kissed her on the cheek and said he would come back to get me after work. That was my last day alone with her.

Several days later, the oncologist informed Dad there was no hope left for my mother. She was dying.

An oncology nurse told us that Mommy was going to hold on as long as we were there, but as soon as we left, she would pass on. Dad made the difficult decision for all of us to leave. We each said our goodbyes to her as we kissed those once chubby cheeks with him being the last one to say his goodbyes. We left the room, so only God knows what he said. The drive home was tortuously slow and she was right, she would never see the house again.

We were home less than an hour when the hospital called to inform Dad that his Sweet Lorraine had died.

My mom was the strongest woman I have ever known. Throughout her health challenge, she always displayed grace and was always concerned about her family.

I thank God for allowing me to participate in her journey. Not knowing at the time, but looking back, I see God's loving hand in every step leading to her home going. I see how the Lord has given me a sensitive, caring spirit and undeniable strength to overcome my own personal health challenges.

"For the Lord is good and his love endures forever;
his faithfulness continues through all generations."
— Psalm 100:5

Angela Patterson is a Registered Nurse/ Case Manager by profession. At the age of 25 she gave her life to the Lord. She has gone through many personal trials and health challenges but her love for Jesus and strong faith has made her more than a conqueror. She has shared her heart so that other women would find inspiration from her journey.

≫ CHENISE PAYTON ≪

Young Love Experience

Young Love Experience

*W*hat is young love? I remember when I first met my husband at a graduation party. At that time, he was a guy at the party. I never imagined us getting married. He is always reminiscing about him asking my two friends to dance with him before he would ask me.

Then, it was my turn. While dancing, he asked me, "Do, you want to take a walk outside?"

Usually, I would have declined, but this felt different, and, for reasons unknown at that time, I felt safe to answer, "Yes. Why not? I will take a walk with you."

We walked around the neighborhood, laughing, talking, and looking at houses. Back then, it was safe to walk around Chicago, Illinois neighborhoods. Times were different then; violence was not at an all-time high as it is today. During our walk, we enjoyed sharing our opinions: what we liked and disliked about each house, or what we would change. We were enjoying each other's conversation.

My attraction has always been to inward first and then outward appearance. The world is concerned about the outward and not inward appearances. When we gather with our friends, the first questions asked are about how they look, dress, or if they smell good. Being young and in love, we think our thinking is correct. Who can tell us about our feelings? Yes, we all experience first love, second love, or maybe even third love and beyond, but it's unlikely it will be our last love. The emotional experiences are real. It doesn't matter how old you are when you felt the feeling, love is real.

We continued seeing each other. At the age of sixteen, while this relationship was another added to my list, it was nothing serious. After a couple weeks went passed, we were talking on the phone every day and after school. We did not have a dull moment. Still, I was not taking him seriously. At some point, I briefly talked to another boy at school. On one particular day, this same guy came over my house unexpectedly. Although it was purely platonic, my parents were old school; they did not believe in boy's holding up company at the house. They believed in being in the house before the street lights came on, before you could go outside or even ask to go anywhere, your homework and chores had to be done, no unnecessary television watching and my bedtime was 10:00 p.m. Somehow, I was able to convince them to change their minds, even though they had strict rules. Nevertheless, this boy had the same nickname as my boyfriend (whom I eventually married). While he was over my house, the phone rang and I answered it. It was my boyfriend. The boy grabbed the phone and asked, "Who is this?" My boyfriend responded with his nickname, and the boy as unsure of what he had said. I grabbed the phone and threw him out my house. Afterwards, my boyfriend came over. He did not understand what had happened either. I surely didn't want that to happen again. That situation was crazy. We were able to get past the confusion and made up.

My boyfriend started taking our relationship seriously, which caused me to feel that maybe he was the one for me. I started rethinking my list. He was caring and showed different interests than the average guy. I'm only sixteen years old, and I know nothing about relationships or marriage, but as every little girl wants to be married, have kids and live happily ever after like a fairy tale story, so did I.

My desire of being married came true on Saturday, August 18, 1990 with this special guy I met at a graduation party. We have been married for twenty-six years and have one adult son. We have been through some testing times, but God is continuing to keep us, and our marriage. I can look back and embrace every tested time that was designed to prepare us for His glory and purpose in our life, and to be a true testimony of God's plan. As I reflect, it was not easy and times were hard, but we had to learn to walk by faith and believe God had our backs.

Being married at the age of twenty and he was twenty-one, and having our first son which he was 16 months, we were young and wet behind our ears. I recall a conversation I had with my deceased mother-in-law weeks before the wedding.

"What do you know about love?" she asked me.

I answered, "We love each other and want to get married."

Now, I honestly can say, we did not have a clue about love at our age. Of course, your first thought is that it is special, and you never felt this feeling with anyone else before. Young love can be an intense feeling.

Being a young adult is time for fun and growth, and not getting married. Most young adults probably think parents or older adults do not understand them. Now I realize, looking back over my teenage years, my parents were teenagers before becoming adults, too. They might have experienced some of the things I experienced during my teenage or young adult years. Being a young and married in our twenties, our young love was up for the challenge of life.

Statistically, we should have not been able to rise above the odds we had against us as a married, young, Black couple in our early twenties with one child. We were able to triumph and achieve some of our goals. He completed four years of the United States Navy as a Mess Management Specialist Cook, which he managed thirteen kitchen staffs aboard the USS New Jersey Battleship in preparing a variety of meals for all different groups up to several hundred for the Officers and Commanding Officer Mess.

As for myself, I've completed my Bachelor's in Computer Science, and continued furthering my education by obtaining a Master's in Business Administration.

Always, believe you have to work hard to obtain what you want out of life. It could be love, education, parenthood, relationship or friendship; no matter what obstacle might stand in your way of life, you can rise above the situation.

Chenise Payton has been married over twenty years and has one son. She is the author of Young Love Experience *and a graduate of University of Phoenix with her Master's Degree in Business Administration. Furthermore, she holds a Bachelor's Degree in Computer Information System with years of exposure in the field. She loves to encourage others by helping them to see the best in themselves, which is why she became a Professional Certified Christian Life Coach. This comes natural to her.*

≫ SHIRLEY POITIER ≪

Fear

Fear

*H*er hair was dirty strawberry blond, her energy nervous, and her assignment: to upset me. This young woman attended a special day program for special needs adults just south of San Francisco. I wanted you to know her because I learned a "don't let it happen" life lesson with her that blustery morning I recall almost every day since.

Let me set you up with the rest of the scene. She walked into the loud and busy lobby. Her eyes zoned in to meet mine. She saw it—FEAR—everything that makes me cry, all of that icky stuff baked on to my heart, that feeling just before my heart muscle squeezes real tight, and the sweat on my brow beads. I had it; she saw it…I wasn't ready for her that morning. Had it overtaken me, would I lose this fight, were they jumping me like a good gang-banging initiation? Or, worse yet, a housewife's fist fight. Nope, not at all because what this really was, was a lifelong lesson because here goes the Teacher (Holy Spirit) now breaking it down for me as simple as a mathematical addition problem from kindergarten.

She grabbed me around the neck, stepped on my boot, and grabbed my other hand and squeezed it with a hard and steady pulse. She growled and put her head close to mine. I was thinking she was going to head-butt me on top of all this. She grinned as if to say, "I have you!" (What is so deep is that she was non-verbal and saying so much voiceless.) She appeared to have a relentless pursuit to destroy me there; right in front of staff, and her peers. The staff was singing in unison a choir melody: "Let her go. Let her go." Her laughter increased as the tension swelled. What was happening to me? Fear was fighting me as it always did—every day, every hour, maybe every minute.

Admittedly, I was unready, yet ready to fight if I had to. I placed my feet firmly on the ground while taking my hands out of my pockets. I had a hypeman like Flava Flav in my ear: "Yeah, girl." Let's just say my mind took a U-turn: I was ready to push her off, knuckle up, grab her hair and start with the upper cuts. The voice that is usually faint was clear: "Push her off you." She can't do this now, here, again: No, I ain't afraid of you! Or what you represent...

I go to my car, checked to see if anyone was looking, put my head in the palm of my hand, took a deep breath and said, "God what just happened to me?"

I heard Him say, "I took a vivid Polaroid (*perhaps a Snap Chat?*) in the flesh of that ugly demon that follows you all day long..."

I say to Him faintly, "I am not afraid of her or the things that come for me anymore."

"What changed?" He asked.

"I went from blind to seeing...I could see her moves...I could see her distain of me...I see that I am stronger than her. My mind is swift... my voluptuous body has Wonder Woman powers... I have Peace as my doorkeeper. I win whether I am fighting or standing still. Thank you for showing me how to stand up to her. How to ready my feet. How to listen to that voice that says fight. How to shake the devil off."

When I look back at the war (because I know I have to be strategic about this thing), I lay it all out on the table as though I am in the Situation Room at the White House. I have to prepare for an attack again because I know they will return for blood. But first, who is my enemy? Where is the enemy? And what am I going to do to defeat this fool?

I know that my enemy is myself—the part of me that does not trust God. It's also that "thing" out there that wants to snuff out my light. The light that makes those in darkness uncomfortable with me. It's the contrasting color God uses to color my life to reveal the true star. Where is the enemy? It's in my thoughts, my dreams, and yes in my hopes for the future. How do I conquer him/her/them? Yes, wait for it…I trust my Creator. I surrender and fight at the same time like shifting a stick shift clutch. I breathe in the moment as it lends me power. It pumps oxygen into my system as though I am rebooting my computer with an update.

I don't even have to say it with my words. It shows in my being. It does not open the door or, in this case, make eye contact with the predator. I walk in the priceless peace that has been given to me with a receipt that is paid in full. I float like a butterfly, and sting like my brother, Ali, said. I straighten my crown with each step and I say to this foolish fear: "I ain't scared of you." If you come back tomorrow I will be here with a clear mind, my discernment in tack, my stilettos to the ground and my earrings off. Let me state it to you again: "Fear, I ain't afraid of you," —Bernie Mac

So now my contender, my opponent, the distractor, the discourager has to think twice before approaching me. As it now knows, I will fight back. I am wiser now, stronger now! I say to those of you who are jumped continuously, review my recipe daily and don't be afraid anymore.

Here is the recipe again, in case you missed it...L.I.F.E

L—Look at the fear head on—don't pretend it is
   not there~ never substitute DENIAL in this
   recipe
I—Inspect it-look up and down and try to figure
   how it got there, who sent it and why?
F—Fight it no matter if it is spiritual, emotional or
   physical—use your pre strategic plans at any cost
E—Exhale—Breathe Deeply ~ Remembering this
   too shall pass.

*"Be strong and courageous. Do not be afraid or
terrified because of them, for the Lord God goes with
you, he will never leave you or forsake you"*
— Deuteronomy 31:6

A daughter of the King, wife, mother, sister and friend, Shirley is a lover of all things funny and never says no to a good belly laugh. A native Californian, she takes pride in living in the heart of Silicon Valley and is full of life stories that reveal God in big and small ways. Shirley is a soul care practitioner whose heart's passion is to help someone along the way. Deeply loved by the Father, she in turn loves deeply: Enjoy her stories in BGV (Black Girl Version, of course)!

≫ PHYLLIS POWELL ≪

Not Perfect, Just Parents

Not Perfect, Just Parents

I was in my twenties when I really gained appreciation for my parents. I also realized during that time they were not super human, they were only human. They did many things right and some wrong. I am not a parent, but I know parenting does not come with a handbook. As I grew older, I gained more of an understanding of the sacrifices they made for my sister and me. As I gained this knowledge, I realized growing up I took them for granted. My parents were not perfect, but they were very good to us and to others. Both worked hard, were not abusive, and provided for us the way parents should. I know having great parents is a blessing not given to everyone. They did their best and taught us the basics for being good people.

When I was born, I lived on the west side of Chicago. Uprooted from the first grade midyear I was catapulted into a new reality. I remember not wanting to leave my friends, but a six –year- old has no say in where they live. My parents moved us to the far north side of Chicago. They wanted better lives for us all. This move afforded us access to better schools, and the neighborhood was a far cry from where we had come.

I imagine relocating was not easy for them. All their family and friends lived more than forty-five minutes away, and we spent a lot of time with our grandparents and other family members. We moved solely for the benefit of my sister and me. Our new school was as diverse as you could get. Most of my friends, both Black and White had parents who were immigrants. Still, there were not a significant number of Black families. Lucky for us, the diversity spared us of feeling any different from our peers. We dealt with little racism and fought when we had to in order to gain respect. Our parents supported us in our transition in every way they could. The first year was challenging for us.

Thinking back, my parents went above and beyond to show us love. The second summer after our move, we went to camp at the Off the Street Club. My mother's friend ran the program and it was specifically for underprivileged children. We were not dirt poor, but expensive summer camps were not an option. My parents also decided they wanted us to have more exposure to the Black culture, so what better way than to send us to a camp that catered to Black youth. The camp was located in Wheaton Illinois, which was about an hour-and-a half from our home. We spent a week a camp. As a seven year old painfully shy child, I had some difficulty being away from my folks. Our only means of communication was writing and a pay phone, as cell phones were nonexistent.

At camp, my sister and I were individuals. Although she looked out for me, she had her own thing going on. My sister was nine and was the social butterfly of the camp. As I followed behind my friends, she became the leader of many packs. She excelled at swimming, dancing and even archery. However, I was the baby of the family and I missed my folks like crazy. I ultimately became independent that summer and learned that our parents went beyond the duty of showing us love.

One day I was swimming in the pool and to my surprise, my father surfaced right next to me. He had driven the hours ride from work, with his swim trunks in tow. That began many trips he made to camp to check on us. His shift at Ford Motors ended at 2:30p.m. He would arrive by 3:30 p.m., and do whatever activity with us that was going on and be making the hour-and-a –half ride home between 5:30 p.m. or 6 .pm. My dad was a huge man, so we were the least bullied kids at that camp. I loved his visits which sometimes occurred at least three out of the seven days we were there. We attended camp every other week, so it was not like he had not seen us. Even now, we often joke that he went away to camp.

During the Fourth of July while at camp, my sister and I were called away from the pool and were told to dress and report to the dining hall. Angry and confused the two of us stomped our way to the mess hall. When we arrived, our parents were there with an entire table filled with food. They had brought us the entire Fourth of July dinner. The dinner consisted of ribs, chicken, burgers, and all the trimmings for the meal. Although embarrassed, we sat as a family and had a great dinner. We were eight and ten and in our two summers there, I never saw a single parent show up other than ours.

When my sister graduated from eighth grade, she saw a prom dress in a magazine. She wanted the dress badly, but my mom could not find it. My father saw the dress and found the pattern for it. My dad was a man of many talents and I had forgotten he had tailoring skills. Although he had not made anything in my lifetime, he cleaned off our old sewing machine and went to work. The love for a child is a strong motivation. The dress was identical to the one in the magazine and she LOVED it!

My mother was equally amazing in showing her love for us. Funny how you think all moms are as awesome as yours. When

I accidentally stepped on and killed a sparrow I was nursing back to health, she assisted my friends and me with the funeral services. I was ten and she even gave me a sympathy card and prepared snacks for the repast. All my friends loved her because she nurtured and loved them. Mom could always tell which of my friends needed some love and easily shared hers with them.

Mom often made elaborate lunches for my friends. Our neighbors looked out for us, as did our parents for their kids. We were the epitome of an American family in a great neighborhood. I often reflect on the good times we spent together as a family. Many times, even in my teens, I preferred the company of my parents than hanging out in the streets with my friends. However, there were bad times too.

By the age of sixteen, my sister had become a bit of a wild child. She was definitely still a leader, but became a saver of lost souls. This resulted in her dating one of the most troubled teens in the school. His name was Dwayne and he was from a broken family. His mother was raising him and his brother on her own, but she was not the nurturing mother one would want. She did not work and ran the streets with any and all sorts of men. Dwayne had quite a reputation as a bad boy, and a criminal record a mile long. What his mother could not provide, he took from others, but my sister saw only the good in him.

During the summer of 1977, we were to make our yearly jaunt to Florida to visit Dad's family. Mom did not make the trip as she could not get the time off. Prior to leaving, my keys came up missing. I say missing because I am a creature of habit and seldom misplace anything. The day they went missing, I dreamt my keys were stolen, and our home was being robbed. The day before we left, my keys magically appeared in the chair Dwayne was sitting in while visiting. I adamantly insisted my parents change the locks immediately. I told them about my vivid dream and was in tears as I tried to convince them it was a premonition. My thirteen –year-old voice fell on deaf ears and the second day in Florida we received word we had been robbed. Fortunately, my mom was not present, but everything of value was stolen. My folks worked hard for the small luxuries we had and my Dad was livid. All of his expensive stereo equipment was stolen as well. Of course, we knew who had done it as there was no forced entry.

Dad had my sister invite Dwayne over for dinner which was not usual as mom had fed him many a day. Told to make myself scarce, I returned two hours later to friends from the building cleaning blood from the walls in the hallway. I ran up to the third floor as quickly as my legs would allow and no one was there. When I asked our friends what had happened, they said Dad had shot Dwayne!

As it turned out during dinner Dad confronted Dwayne and kindly asked for the return of the stolen items. When Dwayne got smart and disrespectful, Dad commenced to pistol whipping him and the gun discharged shooting Dwayne in the head. He lived, but only because of my Mom's quick thinking of clotting the blood with cold compresses. Dad's coaching by the police caused his immediate release from jail. Since Dwayne had such an extensive criminal record, the story was that Dad shot him while he burglarized our home.

When my family returned late that night, I saw my Dad cry for the first time. He was devastated that he had succumbed to his anger enough to harm someone. As a family, we discussed the events and consoled each other. He explained that his actions not only almost killed Dwayne, but also could have easily destroyed our family. He told us that "things" were replaceable but people were not. He apologized for sacrificing his family for material things. That night, we bonded even more as a family and talked until almost dawn.

Dwayne lost his eye as a result of the shooting. When we returned to school, he took to terrorizing my sister until my cousins took care of that issue. Shortly after they roughed him up he dropped out of school. Our near perfect family now had a flaw. In all honesty, we all would have benefitted from some therapy. Black folks seldom seek out psychological assistance when they need it. Instead, we leaned on each other for support. Dad told us he forgave Dwayne and so should we. We discussed what may have led him to robbing us and prayed for his healing.

For many years after, it was as if Dwayne had dropped off the face of the earth. It was twenty years later when I saw him again. I was picking up a meal from a neighborhood restaurant. As I was leaving, I collided into him. I was hoping he did not recognize me until he said my name. Awkward would not quite describe how I felt, as I had never had any correspondence with him after the shooting. After exchanging quick pleasantries, Dwayne told me he was working with troubled youths. He explained how the shooting saved him as it set him on the right path to helping others. He also told me to tell my father that he forgave him long ago.

I'm sure the shooting changed my Dad but ultimately made him more compassionate. My mother's undying love and support was the glue to our family. They taught us love, respect, and forgiveness. For this, I am eternally grateful God chose them for me.

Phyllis Powell is a retired City of Chicago employee. She has a B.A. in Political Science from Loyola University, Chicago. Having worked for the past thirty years, she is enjoying the freedom to travel and looking forward to future endeavors.

≫ GABRIELA RIVERO ≪

From Venezuela to Chicago
An Impossible Dream Made Possible

From Venezuela to Chicago
An Impossible Dream Made Possible

*N*eglect and lack of education, stability, direction, and money made my dream of coming to the United States of America to learn English, and becoming a U.S. citizen an impossible one.

This dream was so difficult to reach; when I mustered the confidence to tell people I was going to the USA to learn English, some told me, with honesty, to "stop dreaming" and "get real." Others looked at me with pity, knowing for sure it would be easier to see pigs flying than to see me going to the USA.

A well-respected friend of the family said, "You've gotta stop being so immature and be more like your sister Lilian, who is very mature. How do you plan to go there? There is no way you are going to ever go there. Just stay at your job and stop dreaming about pigs flying," and shook his head.

For many years, I had forgotten about my dream and did what he recommended, but the deep desire to leave Venezuela for the United States would not leave me alone. To worsen matters, my mother didn't want to hear the words: The United States in my mouth and threatened to hit me in the mouth and make me swallow my teeth like pills.

The facts and realities were enough to justify people's skepticism. I listened to them, let the experts deter my dream, and went about my life. Then, one day, a song in English played on the radio and ignited a deep longing, this voice from afar calling me to come over. I decided to do it and things aligned for me to make the trip.

My first memory of the world, the memory of my existence, was when I was four years old. My family relocated to the Panama border. My parents had ended their relationship and were moving to Tanela, a small town of two hundred people. We were traveling by canoe, and little green leaves were lurking on the surface of the water, like pirates attacking the little canoe.

After that long journey via canoe, we walked for many days since there were no cars or horses to take us there. As we walked through the thick jungle, carrying suitcases and God knows what else. When we stopped to rest, the men cut plantain leaves and made them into the shape of cups that looked like Dixie cups and used them to scoop water from the rivers to drink. Sometimes my grandmother told us, "Cover your feet because there are snakes." I was terrified of snakes then, and still terrified to this day. After days of walking back to another canoe surrounded by water, we arrived to Tanela. Everything seemed stable. My mother had met one of the locals, they married, and we had a stepdad. He seemed nice, except on the days when he beat my pregnant mother, who was expecting her fifth child.

These memories are like old movies that come and go, but there is one memory that will be with me forever: my mother holding my and my brother's, Eduard's, hands as we climbed into another small canoe. Raging waters moved so fast, it seemed like the canoe had no ability to stay steady, the wild river and my little brother's fear, the rapid water shaking our little canoe and threatening to take our lives. That day, my mother had left two of her small children behind: one-year-old Eliuth and two-year-old Lilian, who screamed and called out my name, asking me to come back. I still feel the pain. At such young age, I couldn't understand the pain my mother was feeling. At twenty-five years old, she already had five children and for circumstances she doesn't share, she had to leave them behind.

Mother was a very restless woman. We settled in Cartagena, a coastal city in Colombia, but she became restless again and, at the first opportunity she had, she left for Venezuela and left behind an eleven-month-old baby, a six-year-old boy, and eight-year-old me. Suddenly, I found myself living with strangers and taking care of a baby. This family could have cared less about us. Left behind with strangers, I had the responsibility of taking care of my little sister like an adult.

A few months later, my stepdad came and took my little sister and brother to his mom's, and left me in the house with strangers who didn't want me around. Up to that point, I had always been a very cheerful person. Despite all the moves, lack of stability, poverty, neglect, and losses, I was a very optimistic child. However, this experience was the one that, for the first time, made me feel deep sadness and anger.

For the next five years, I lived in five different houses until Mother took us to Caracas, Venezuela, a few months after my thirteenth birthday.

When I was fifteen years old, we met Marina and Mario, or, as we called them Mario-and-Marina, as if they were one person. We always said their names in one breath. This young couple changed my life without realizing it. Marina was a young woman of eighteen and Mario was twenty-two. Marina was Venezuelan and Mario was a Cuban-born police officer, whose mother had lived in Miami for many years.

Mother worked part-time in a furniture store. She was a very interesting person. Even though she was very abusive and neglectful to us, she was very kind to strangers. She met Mario and Marina at the furniture store the day Marina's father threw them out of his house.

One afternoon, Mother showed up with the young couple. Marina, a tall, dark-skinned woman, with long, wavy, silky hair down to her waist, was so beautiful. She irradiated so much kindness that I loved her instantly. I wanted her to be my big sister. Mario was not as tall, but very handsome. They adjusted to our one-bedroom house very quickly.

Life with Marina and Mario was one of the happiest times of our lives. Mario being a police officer helped a lot. During the month they lived in our house, waiting for their visa to go to Miami, was one of the happiest months of my life. Marina helped me a lot, doing chores around the house, and Mother was very careful not to hit me in front of a police officer. I was her favorite punching bag. Mario and Marina became so fond of me that they promised that as soon they settled down, they would send for me. Of course, Mom said, "No," and I said, "No."

For the next few years, they continue writing, but like most people who leave, they adapted to their new life and forgot those they left behind. Marina sent us a picture of her in Miami with little Mario. She looked so beautiful and radiant. We never responded to her letters. I was too busy trying to save myself from the next beating from my mom. However, this short interaction with Mario and Marina sparked something in me that never turned off. I would forget about it at times, but then one day there was a little voice that whispered to me, "Let's go to the USA." The dream to come to the USA and learn English kept me alive and sane during difficult times in my life when I didn't want to be alive anymore. This dream of starting a new life under my own terms and being my own woman, gave me the strength to keep going and have faith.

I had never thought about the USA as a possibility in my life. The idea of starting in a new country as a foreigner was not very appealing to me. Adapting to this new country as a teenager had already been a very difficult transition. However, once this desire grabbed hold of me, like glue, it was impossible to shake it off. This wild and almost impossible dream started with Marina and Mario's arrival to our house. They sparked my desire, and didn't even know it.

In 1977, we arrived in Caracas Venezuela from the flat coast of Cartagena, where it was hot and dry, and ninety degrees, to the hills of Caracas with an average morning temperature of sixty degrees. I remember walking up those hills, feeling like I couldn't breathe. My skinny body could feel every bit of the cold cutting through my bones like a knife. The entire family settled in a very poor area in Caracas called Plan de Manzano. My stepdad built a very rustic house for us to live in and we all had to share the same room. As we got older, I started working at a bank, my brother, Eduard, started working at a race horse magazine, and as soon as we felt established at work, we convinced our parents to leave the hills and move to a better neighborhood. It took time to convince them, but they finally came with us to see the apartment my brother and I had found, and they signed the lease since my brother and I were too young to sign it.

Tragedy struck our family in December 1987 when my brother tragically passed. I was in such deep pain that I left the bank and became more serious about my dream to go to the United States. After I made the decision, and I *knew* I was going no matter how long it took me, I relaxed. I started to focus on the task at hand with diligence and excitement. I didn't know how or how long it would take before I could make my move, but somehow, it was going to happen. I started to save money and continued learning English.

Like guided by God, I started working as a secretary for an American company. There I met four angels, with whom I shared my dream and two of them helped me get to America. I arrived in Chicago on February 19, 1992 from Caracas, with average temperature of sixty to eight-five degrees to Chicago's twenty degrees the day that I arrived.

Besides commitment, action and faith, I knew the allotted time I had to accomplish my goal. When I came to the U.S., my visa expired in a year so I had a great sense of urgency and focus; I knew I had to go return to Venezuela in a year. Therefore, I left my house every day at 7:30 a.m., arrived to school at eight, and stayed until seven. I listened to tapes, read, used my dictionary (there was no Google at that time), and immersed myself one hundred percent in the language. I became friends with people from other countries to force myself to speak English, even though I was barely able to understand it or speak it, but I stayed focused. I made the decision to stay away from my tribe of Spanish speakers because I had that deadline and I knew I was not going to be able to achieve my goal and learn English if I didn't muster the courage of being seen as an "arrogant Latina" and do what I was supposed to do.

Looking back at my life and its ups and downs, I have found that the times in my life when things worked out was when I detached myself from the results and said, "God, Your will not mine," and trust that His will is always wiser and better than mine.

Reflecting on my life as a child and as an adult coming from situations where my percentage of success was very low, there have been qualities I call the four virtues that have been my guiding light: a childlike innocence, commitment which ignites focus, faith and gratitude. I don't know how or when I welcomed them as part of my existence, but now that I have become more aware, I cannot live without them. A child's innocence opens a world of possibilities when things seem impossible and allows that child to dream. Commitment ignites the focus and the responsibility to do what is my part to do. Faith in self and in a higher power guides me to meet the angels that open doors for me. Gratitude is the flame that keeps the rest alive for when I forget to be like an innocent child and see possibilities, forget my commitments to please others and put others dreams above mine, lose faith in myself and God in moments in my life when I lost my brother, when I got divorced, lost my homes, etc. I stop for a second and in the midst of my pain, I know I have so much already, and gratitude helps me smile, laugh, and see possibilities again.

As I got older, my goals and needs changed. My highest goal is to love everyone and everything, starting with myself. When I reflect on my life and the people that lived in my neighborhood, I could say that my possibilities to come to the USA from the hills of Caracas were probably 1 in 50,000. I am grateful for these experiences. I wonder how my life would have turned out without them.

For many years, I was angry at my mother for leaving me behind and for the abuse and neglect I suffered during those years at the hand of the people she entrusted to take care of me. However, after many years, I became a mother and grew tired of my own anger. One day I asked myself, *if my mom was not my mother and that woman had had the childhood my mother had, how would I feel toward that person?* My mother suffered so much and faced a lot of abuse and neglect, but she was better than my grandmother. My grandmother was probably better than her own mother. As I remember now, how life was like living with my grandmother the few times I did, I cried for my mother. As a deep feeling of compassion filled my heart, I decided to forgive her and forgive my father for not being there for us. I realize that I can't change the past no matter how much I try. I can only create my today every day with my attitude and faith that God is there for me. God has opened doors for me that seemed impossible for me to open, that is why, one of my favorite Bible verses is, *"With God all things are possible."*

Through the years, my mom and I have become good friends. Forgiveness is an active and constant job. There are days I still become angry with her, but I remind myself that fighting the past only brings me suffering and I choose today. I still carry the scars of my childhood, but they remind me in difficult moments that I am a strong woman, that I am a survivor, that I am not alone. I see my mom's face deepened with so much sorrow as she carries her own scars, but I choose to give that burden to God and I choose to honor her scars and mine because those scars remind me of how wonderful life can become. At times when I forget my dreams and become lost for a while I know that I can always start again.

Gabriela Rivero is originally from Colombia and raised in Venezuela. She is a Christian coach, Passion Test Facilitator and a Prayer Chaplain at Unity in Chicago.

❊❊ NORMIA VÁZQUEZ SCALES ❊❊

Until Further Notice

Until Further Notice

*T*he temperature blazed amid the city, prompting Floridian natives to plunge into the watery deep oceanic expanse. The haze and shade became progressively pronounced, as the background deepened to highlight the iridescent medal voguing in the whistling heights. Meanwhile, I whisked through the opaque French doors embossed with dusky pink script, shed my Enzo Angiolini stilettos and slithered into Lotus pose. Jenna's mindful declaration permeated the consciousness of fellow members of the Yoga session inclusive of me. Hence, I vividly recall her eloquently executed lesson on the topic of inevitable impermanence, which I readily embraced.

Upon skimming my retrospective and customized "book of life," I've ingested and digested the core concept of impermanence as I've incessantly spoken upon with grace and due comfort. Rather than campaigning against impermanence or change, I succumb and extract its benevolence and instructions, nevertheless. Just as humans and water physically undergo their respective metamorphoses, so does the intangible.

Personally, I can attest to this via my Three Great Ones, none other than my utmost stellar romantic relationships bestowed in the wake of my young adulthood. Each pairing conclusively yielded a water-colored storybook romance, to say the least. Every love-drenched letter, verbal Tango, and rendezvous between state lines apparently crystallized each of the aforementioned long-distance relationships until impermanence surfaced. This time, it bore the guise of deceit, betrayal and loneliness, which compromised the foundation of each union. What I'd mutually forecasted as infinitely unshakable, impermeable bonds had become negated. Not merely once, not twice, but thrice. Yet, I prevailed despite my heartache and devastation.

The recurring anthem, impermanence, eclipsed again amid my former marriage projected as my "happily ever after," via my then husband's extramarital affair with controlled substances, which mutilated our bond. Despite my agony, fever and grief, I channeled the strength to execute "the Gift of Goodbye." Moreover, I siphoned the good from this tumultuous chapter: God's divine favor, grace, protection and my eternal gratitude, coupled with my dearest son, Máximo.

How often has one vowed to themselves to, "Never... (fill in the blank)?" In fact, how many times have we committed to what I classify as a final destination? Well, I personally concur with both of the aforementioned. Aside from my marital chapter as illustrated previously, I recall my collegiate experience. In laymen's terms, I had a made up mind to pursue and acquire my Metallurgical Engineering degree *exclusively* from the Illinois Institute of Technology (IIT). However, my fond friend and foe, impermanence, miraculously materialized, thereby altering my fate. Nevertheless, I pivoted out of IIT/Engineering and sank into the arms of DePaul University and the realm of Communications. Yet, I savor the effervescent memories and feats throughout that expedition.

"Ahhhhhh!" I smile inwardly, as I reminisce upon commencing from my alma mater and plunging into the iridescent waters of freelance Photojournalism (indeed another publicly declared career destination), only to pirouette into the arenas embodying: American Trans Air, Dyson Inc., Florida State University, Miami-Dade Public Schools, The US Department of Commerce, and Chapel Hill-Carrboro City Schools. Yes, the cosmic storm of impermanence appeared in my career sector, prompting me to defy thyself once again. In most instances, my former employers held the autonomy of stamping my expiration date with their empires. As a result, I was forced to surrender to involuntary dismissal from their establishments, despite the blood, sweat and tears I'd shed per each monumental cause. Once again, I avulsed the lesson, which sparked me to erect my existing entrepreneurial Dynasty.

The same impermanence holds true for my residential history—cartwheeling from the bowels of Englewood Chicago, strutting down to temperate/zesty Miami, Florida (a presumed final stop I thought I'd never outgrow), tumbling into the calm of Eden, North Carolina prior to back flipping to Chicago post-separation before ultimately nose diving into the pristine and tranquil confines of Chapel Hill, North Carolina. Instead of soaking in dismay, I acquired carpe diem ideology and proceeded gracefully from episode to episode when necessary.

Impermanence As of Late

The scarlet glare emanating from my Note 5 hosting the breaking news medium ripped me from my comatose slumber.

Thus, I'd been abruptly cast into a sea of bewilderment upon devouring the harsh pill of an incredulous presidential score for the Republican entity. I wallowed in the aura of perplexity, which held me captive, imprisoned, dumbfounded on November 9, 2016. Astonishment transcended to empathy, and empathy morphed into a whirlwind of mourning and betrayal upon digesting the anguish of the impending threat: the annihilation of an ironclad legacy spawn by God and bestowed to our authentic leader: President Barack Obama.

Melodic harmonies spewed lyrics from Seal's "Dreaming in Metaphors" from amplified speakers throughout the cabin of my German import. This melancholic tune permeated my strained emotions, and the dual edge sword of impermanence seized the stage once more. In this context, impermanence functioned as the vehicle of collective hatred, sexism, misogyny and racism, to name a few. The former atmosphere of cohesiveness ushered forth by rational America's pride and joy, President and Commander-in-Chief, Barack Obama, had become abruptly shattered. "Unity" had been rebuked by his abominable fear-mongering successor: Trumpenstein.

Gloom, doom, darkness, and defeat now circumvented the climate spanning American parameters in lieu of Presidential feats, which reigned over an eight-year interval. Dwindling hope took precedence, therefore strangling the soldered and welded spirit of the USA. Impermanence rendered the evidence of the unconventional physician, President Obama, who martyred to acupuncture the supple skin of a country afflicted with the ill demon of greed. I sobbed uncontrollably upon realizing he toiled tirelessly to spare a land entrenched with lust for dismal power of its sins. Political unrest dominated the land oozing proverbial milk and honey.

Now what has transpired? Here lies the aftermath: A revitalized economy limps while stock plummets to incredulous lows. Melanated people have become doused in paranoia upon the prospect of deportation. The LGBT community, adjacent to women nationwide, stand mortified while gazing at the wall of uncertainty in its naked eyes. Stability has become upset by an astronomical state of flux. A plethora of relationships, including marital unions, have weathered the torrential storm induced by this adversity: the 2016 Presidential election. After all, adversity is the abrasive indicator, which evokes and/or challenges impermanence itself. In some instances, relationships have become reinforced whereas utmost sound unions lie at the threshold of cessation, failure, and unfortunately divorce. Such has become the latest reality by virtue of the turbulent waters caused by political discord. Families, friends, husbands, wives, households, and business relationships severed and/or divided.

Given the state of affairs, many asked, "So how shall we proceed?" Some questioned whether to hold or fold? Feast or endure famine? Fight or flee to international soil? My response is to resume and adopt a synchronized carpe diem perspective, my habitual mode of operation. In my humble opinion, this is *not* an Apocalypse, yet another scenario in which we must emerge from the ashes, remain steadfast in faith, discard fear and simply "move with the cheese," per se. Yet, continue to *rise*. I dare to venture boldly into this night, seize the comet by the tail and resume converting tainted lemons (impermanence) into gourmet lemonade. This is the *universal secret to success* in which I implore to all. Moreover, I extend my utmost gratitude to my best friend, Sheila Hylton de Toro Forlenza, for acquainting me with such a priceless gift. Forever envisioning the desired result: optimal success in every facet, even within chaos itself.

Life genuinely is a storm in which we bask in sunshine at some intervals and are shattered upon the rocks during others. However, we withhold the power to decide how to respond in the face of the storms of adversity, which are inevitable to us all. Rather than retreating, face the storm head-on because rewards rest beyond its calm. My life experiences, coupled with my ex-husband's recent and tragic demise, has emboldened me to trade mediocrity for opulence, and frugality for quality. Yet, my integrity has been fortified by pure intentions and higher consciousness. The educational trials Máximo had been stricken with in tried and true schools we've entrusted, will be resolved by virtue of my spawned epiphany/selfless resolution: incessant travel and a homeschooling endeavor. I've shaken the dust from the my shoulders, as well as my son's, chanted the mantra—carpe diem—and struck and purged the concept of *never* from our thoughts. Instead, replacing it with *until further notice*, as we embark upon new journeys.

Normia Vázquez Scales (Mia) is an active mother and savvy entrepreneur, educator, writer and motivational speaker. Mia passionately advocates and promotes balance to both adults and youth alike via educational mediums such as the nationally renowned AVID Program. However, her comprehensive experience entails Reading/ Language Arts Instruction for Miami-Dade Public Schools coupled with efforts in primary school districts encompassing Illinois and North Carolina, respectively.

Furthermore, Mia's Communications credentialing yielded/ birthed from DePaul University has afforded her the opportunity to serve both DePaul and Florida State Universities. Dyson Inc. also labors as a prior landmark, which enabled her to engage in

International Sales, Marketing and Communications. However, her specialty/niche embodies aiding disadvantaged women and male youth yearning to re-hydrate, reinvent and become reacquainted with their former and reinvented selves. Mia's spare time is torn between travelling alongside her son, Máximo, humanitarian endeavors such as her pro bono "Recalibrating the Scales" teleconference calls and youth advocacy in primary academia.

≫ JUDITH WATKINS ≪

I Forgave and She Forgot

I Forgave and She Forgot

Where do I begin? How do I tell the story of a human being who happens to be my mother? It is important to know about her and our struggle to forgive before she forgot. Mom raised me to be as smart and as kind as I can be. The many years of her teaching my siblings and me to do the right thing, for some reason, the right thing didn't happen for her. This caused me to feel some kind of way when I started having to make decisions for her.

Why does this happen to someone so smart, so educated? Mom de-escalated from independence to depending on her children. Why? How? I just can't understand what happened to her. My confusion turned to anger. The idea of the possibility of my not being able to be who I used to be because I now had to take care of the woman who took care of me. I was now a caretaker. What does that mean anyway? This was not supposed to happen to my mother, my family. Why didn't she tell us she was feeling different? I had so many questions, all I kept bottled up in my head. Until I had the nerve to ask my mother, "Why didn't you tell me?" I even said to my sister, "You're so close to her."

My sister didn't accept our mother's slow memory loss. My brother was just quiet and I was just angry and we were scared.

It took me a long time to calm down. It happened so quickly, I had no time to think about why this was happening to us. Why could she have changed so much, and so fast? How could this have happened to someone that was so educated? I expected her to be around a long time, to continue telling me I should do certain things a certain way.

Then, I remembered the signs: locking her keys in the trunk of her car, or not remembering where she left her purse—sometimes in the back seat of her car, sometimes in the trunk. She always managed to call me to come help her find her keys so she could get home. Sometimes she would come home with dents and scrapes on the side of her car. I would ask her, "Ma, what happened?" She told me she had problems getting off the expressway. There was no need for her to be on the expressway coming home. Another time was when she fell down. The Chicago Transit Authority bus driver was driving by. He stopped, parked the bus, and helped her up off the sidewalk. He noticed she had hurt herself; she was bleeding from her mouth, and a bruise on the forehead. He drove her to the nearest hospital and made sure she received care. Later that day, my sister received a phone call from the hospital to come and pick my mother up. Luckily, we had put a piece of paper in her purse with phone numbers to call in case of emergency. Then there were the many times she accused me of stealing her paychecks or something of value that belonged to her. Often times, we would later find those items because she'd forgotten where she'd placed them. These were the first warnings of something that was not right. Shortly after, she was diagnosed with Alzheimer's. She was in her late fifties.

We began our morning ritual: waking up at 5:00 a.m., sometimes we ate, sometimes not. We'd walk to the Metro train station, take the train, and get off at the Hyde Park stop. I would have to talk her into walking up and down flights of stairs—

sometimes she was afraid, other times she just didn't want to do it. Most mornings I cried. I would beg her, "Be good today, Mom, please." By the time we arrived to the adult daycare center to drop her off, I was so stressed. Still, I carried on; I went to work anyway. Some mornings she wouldn't even get out of the house or get dressed, and I had to call someone to care for her, and to take her to the adult daycare center. I would get a call from whoever was caring for her, telling me she wouldn't do anything. In the background, I would hear her, fussing and cursing. I would talk to her as she used to talk to me when I acted out as a child.

I was so frustrated, sad, depressed, and overwhelmed. I asked God, "Why? Why am I caring for someone who really didn't like me?" We always argued and saw things differently. Then I would remember my grandmother's words: *Be there for family no matter what, you're the oldest and the strongest.* My grandmother was my first best friend. I continued and began to cry more, but never stopped being there for my mom.

I moved into the bedroom across from Mom's room. One night, I found her lying on the floor next to my bed, so I started sleeping in the same bed with Mom in her room. Every night she would talk to me about what she could still remember. Sometimes would be the same stuff, but I got used to it. One night she was different, more agitated than usual.

"Hey, I have something to tell you," she said to me.

"What is it, Ma?"

She asked me to get closer to her. We were lying in bed, on our sides, face-to-face.

"You're my best child, and the strongest, just like my mama. I am sorry how I treated you." She closed her eyes and went to sleep.

I lay there awake, not knowing how to respond. I had felt so cheated out of my life, being her caretaker, and sometimes her mother, her teacher, and the person she lashed out at and caused harm to—the bruises, scratches, blackened eye. I was so tired and still angry for her putting me in this situation.

Then something came over me.

A voice said, "Stop! She does not know why all this happened. She is confused and angry, too. She's scared and asking the same questions as you are. 'Why am I being punished? Why me?' When her thoughts are clear, she's thinking, *I don't deserve my oldest child to care for me because I have been so harsh to her for so long.*"

Just then, Mom's eyes opened. She looked at me and said, "Thank you for being so patient, responsible, and strong hearted. I love you, my baby."

Words could not describe how I felt hearing those words. I cried like a baby for hours.

Night turned to day, Mom woke up, and we start our routine. However, this morning, she was her worse.

I forgave her and she forgot everything we discussed. I was okay because I didn't forget. Soon after friends and family slowly stop calling or coming by to visit. She forgave them and they forgot her.

A native of Chicago, Illinois, Judith Watkins loves helping people, especially children, even when she spent time out of the country on military assignment. She enjoys telling stories, most of which are true, and sometimes with a funny twist. As the eldest of three children, I have made my brother and sister laugh so many times, even when they didn't want to. I am still a caretaker, caring for my dad and family. This would be my first time writing, so I hope you enjoy.

≫ VELMA WHITE ≪

Broken, Out of Nothing, Came Something!

Broken, Out of Nothing, Came Something!

Early Childhood

A significantly glorious flower, the Magnolia—in spite of Mississippi's horrific history of bloodshed of African Americans—the state's flower is glorious as it falls from the Magnolia tree. Vera was born in Mississippi and loves the sweet aroma from the magnolia flowers as she walks on a dusty country road. School ended for the summer and her best friend Renee helped with her math homework. Thank God, Vera made it through her junior year and the last year of math.

In a position of authority, seeds of hate, anger, envy and jealous can be planted by someone. Vera was teased by her teacher because she had 14 siblings. Her teacher laughed in front of the class because she thought her siblings had different parents. Vera was embarrassed. The teacher continued teasing her, because her siblings were different shades of black. Vera never noticed their different skin tones until her teacher embarrassed her. Vera, made it home in tears, she explained to her mom what happened in school. Needless to say, Vera never had any problems with that teacher. Just as seeds of hate can be sowed, seeds of love, joy, peace, trust, wisdom, knowledge, prosperity, and health can empower you. Vera's positive affirmations came from her parents. She never forgot the negative seed planted by her teacher.

Vera struggled with fears for the rest of her life. Most of all taking chances, learning to love and be loved. Like most fairy tales, she believed in knights with shining armor. A man that could love with a pure heart, strong, secure in God and confidence to lead. Like her father, but 6› tall, dark and handsome. As she transitions through life, she married the opposite of her father. She has a 26-year-old beautiful daughter and granddaughter. Vera›s turbulent marriage ended. Vera was from a two-parent home, true love and family values were demonstrated. Her parents loved their children. Yearly, her mom would cook a feasts and family would come as far as Chicago, California & Texas. Feasting on mom's yams, greens, ribs, fried chicken, catfish, baked mac cheese, ham, chitterlings was a treat. Some called it slave food. Be thankful our ancestors were wise enough to take the scraps and make a meal. This was our favorite time of the year. Our city cousins learned country games; hopscotch, rolling tire game and «the war» (males only). This was played with live fireworks! We never lost anyone, a few close calls! Her mom was a stay home mom, played piano and her favorite song, I will let nothing separate me from the love God. Vera admired her parents. Her parents didn›t have much, but they gave to others. Vera watched her mom sacrifice for the love of her family.

Mom's Ultimate Sacrifice!

Vera and her siblings were playing outside. They often rode their bikes, roller skates, played marbles, or searched for old tin to make a slide. They would slide all day. Vera's brother decided to slide down a different hill. Their mom loved her children. Vera listened in Sunday school class about Jesus ultimate sacrifice. Jesus took 183 lashes, His skin ripped from his bones, blood gushed from his body. He was tortured all night. Jesus was pierced in his side, crown made of thorns and placed upon his head. The thorns painfully, pierced through his head. Jesus endured the greatest sacrifice to save us. Vera's mom sacrificed daily for her family. As they were playing, her mom sensed something was wrong. Vera's brother slid down a hill and landed in a thorn tree. He screamed with unbearable pain. Vera was 5, and her brother was 8. She tried to pull him from the thorn tree, he was stuck. He is still screaming. He pleaded to Vera to get his mom. She ran home to get their mom. She heard her son cry. Vera noticed the bump in her mom stomach but she was too young to know her mom was carrying a child. As her mom reach the hill, she realized her son is hurt bad. Their mom coached him through getting untangled, he untangled his leg, his mom asked him to push himself up the hill, he was too weak. Vera noticed her mother looked at her bump in her stomach and into the eyes of her son, within minutes her mom reached down and pulled her son from the thorn tree. Her brother could not walk, blood dripping from his leg. Vera's mom carried him home. Their mom noticed a thorn in his bone she could not pull it out. Their father arrived home and he removed the thorn from her brother's leg. Blood was penetrating through her mom's dress. Later in the night, she could hear her mom moaning from pain, her dad rushed her mom to the hospital. Vera's mom lost her unborn child and saved her living child. The ultimate sacrifice for her son.

Angry with God

Weakness - the state or condition of lacking strength or a quality or feature that prevents someone or something from being effective or useful. What happens when you become angry with God? Ephesians 4:26(KJV) Be ye angry, and sin not: let not the sun go down upon your wrath:

Vera enjoyed teaching *abstinence education*. She brought her daughter along and hoped, she was listening. Her father was a marine, he explained his expectations of her.

Vera's 16-year daughter was scheduled for church camp. However, she backed out. She asks to go to Walmart several times. Vera heard her daughter crying in her sleep. Her daughter finally, told her she took a pregnancy test at Walmart and was pregnant! Vera was extremely upset. How dare my daughter be pregnant at 16? I am an abstinence instructor and how is this possible? *Vera is angry with God*! She chopped down hedge bushes and roots from a tree. God's job was to protect her. She felt the Lord failed her. Her daughter had goals, to finish high school and college. She expected the best for her daughter. Vera researched abortion clinics. The shame attached to teenage pregnancies would be a harsh reality for her daughter. Vera became angrier with God, she even reached out to friends. Don't be fooled by friends that agree with you, when you are wrong. True friends will give you the good, bad and ugly. They wipe tears from your eyes instead of passing you the Kleenex box. They attended a church conference. Her daughter applied the lessons, while Vera was angry and lost for direction. She told her daughter about the abortion appointment. They both stood outside underneath an oak tree. Her daughter stared with disbelief, asked, if she was praying to the same God? God promised, He had forgiven me and that He would take care of me and the baby. I am sorry I disappointed

144

you, but I can't get rid of my baby. Vera realized her daughter made a decision that changed not only her life, but her family and friends. *Vera is* experiencing sleepless nights, as she tossed and turn her eyes are fixed on the night stand clock, the time is 5:55AM. Vera can hear the Lord saying, my great, great, great Grace is sufficient to cover all sins, all will be well. Vera felt the weight lifted, but she had one more hurdle to cross. She needed to inform her daughter's father. He was in the VA hospital, if it did not go well, he was at the best place. The conversation did not go well. He screamed and told them to leave. He eventually, called his daughter told her he loved her, but was disappointed. A few months later, the bundle of joy arrived and everyone forgot about the disappointments. This little girl is just perfect. The Lord promised, Vera all would be well. Grace is now 9 years old, loves God, exceeds academically and in sports. Vera's daughter finished high school, completed MA certification and will graduate from college in 2017.

Many Prayed for Me!

Pray for one another, that ye may be healed. The effectual fervent prayer of the righteous man availeth much, James 5:15. Vera often felted like she was walking alone, especially, when things seemed hard to face. Vera's sisters started a weekly prayer line, after the loss of both parents, brother, nephew and watching her daughter process through losing her father. Vera felt over whelmed. She knew the Lord would not place her in situations, she could not handle. She felt the prayers of many. Vera walked upstairs to her office, she was greeted by the janitor Mrs. Pam. The janitor received the same honor as the Department Dean. Mrs. Pam, loved the Lord, you could see and sense it. Vera walked in her freshly cleaned office, and the prayers covered her. Mrs. Pam's prayers are baked into the walls. She released a victory prayer over Vera, "the Lord called you this season to fulfill his purpose and for you to share with others as the Lord release you. She released a health warning over Vera. Mrs. Pam could hear Vera's difficulties coming up the stairs, she was breathless. She said, Vera, the Lord want you to take your health serious, he is preparing you for an assignment. He wants you to be strong, wise and healthy. Vera, knew this was God using Mrs. Pam.

I am grateful for their prayers.

Election of 2016

My President Barack H. Obama. I remember my dad voting for the first black President in 2008 and my 18-month old granddaughter wearing Obama's 2008 button saying, my Obama! This was an historical moment electing him and to hear my father at 84 years old say, I knew God promised, He would send a promised and he knew it would happen one day, but he did not think it would happen in his life time. My mom, had the chance to voted twice. Black people knew his election fulfilled a promise. I am grateful the Lord allowed him 2 terms. However, my choice for 2016 is Hillary Clinton. Some white people wanted to take their country back. This is God's country. The president elect is drowning in morale decay issues, wife a nude model, disrespecting women, pending rape cases, blacks and Hispanics. The president elect is breaking campaign promises but, they believe they have their country back. They can't match the Obama's integrity or class. Let's pray this scripture, "If my people, which are called by my name, shall humble themselves, and pray, and seek my face, and turn from their wicked ways:

then will I hear from heaven, and will forgive their sin, and will heal their land. (2 Chron. 7:14)

Jesus Carried Me

Vera is older she pondered, how did she make it through sexual abuse at an early age, painful words from her teacher, domestic abuse, divorce and nearly raped by a taxi cab driver. Some people find faith in clinging to their guns. Vera clings to her God. Her mom always said, when things get too hard, pray harder and often. **Perseverance**, is steadfast in doing something despite difficulty or delay in achieving goals. **Psalms 138:8**, The Lord will perfect that which concerneth me; thy mercy Lord, endured forever; forsake not the works of thine own hands. During Vera's quiet time with the Lord, she would pray continuously and God would answer her prayers. One of her old time favorite movie lines, is from Forrest Gump, "life is like a box of chocolate, you never know what you are going to get." In life you may face all kinds of good and difficulties. Keeping God at the Center you can make it through any obstacles.

Victory!

The book of Proverbs reminds us that human preparation is necessary for battle, but we must asks the Lord strategies for battle to gain victory! You can walk in Victory. This does not mean you will not face giants, hardship, and brokenness. The Lord's promise, that whatsoever you shall ask in His name, that will I do, that the Father may be glorified in the Son, if you ask any thing in my name, He will do it, John 14:13-15. Life is a garden, your seeds are your children and the greater seeds could be your parents that have passed on. However, as their seeds flourish in your life and you passed the legacy. Tend to your garden daily, checking the root systems. Jesus is the center! As the seeds develop remove the weeds (the adversaries) do not suffocate your seeds. Vera's garden is her seeds(children) job and family. She prays for wisdom, knowledge, understanding and may her seeds be taught and favored by the Lord. "The world breaks everyone and afterward many are strong at the broken places," Ernest Hemingway. Vera allowed the Lord to mend and restorer all things loss. Victory is mine says, the Lord!

Velma White received her BS from Texas Woman's University. She was born in Batesville, Mississippi, and is the daughter of amazing parents: Reverend Connell and Thelma White. She currently resides in a small town in Texas with her daughter, Veronica, and granddaughter, Jaida. She is a new writer, certified biblical life coach and owner of Victorious Biblical Life Coach, where she coaches clients nationally and internationally.

61748282R00096

Made in the USA
Lexington, KY
19 March 2017